TAKING THE LEAP

BOOKS BY PEMA CHÖDRÖN

Awakening Loving-Kindness

Becoming Bodhisattvas

Comfortable with Uncertainty

The Compassion Book

Living Beautifully

The Places That Scare You

The Pocket Pema Chödrön

Practicing Peace

Taking the Leap

Welcoming the Unwelcome

When Things Fall Apart

The Wisdom of No Escape

TAKING THE LEAP

*Freeing Ourselves
from Old Habits
and Fears*

Pema Chödrön

SHAMBHALA
Boulder
2019

SHAMBHALA PUBLICATIONS, INC.
2129 13th Street
Boulder, Colorado 80302
www.shambhala.com

9 8 7 6 5 4 3

Printed in the United States of America

♾ This edition is printed on acid-free paper that meets the
American National Standards Institute z39.48 Standard.
♻ This book is printed on 30% postconsumer recycled paper.
For more information please visit www.shambhala.com.

Shambhala Publications is distributed worldwide by
Penguin Random House, Inc., and its subsidiaries.

Designed by Lora Zorian

THE LIBRARY OF CONGRESS CATALOGUES THE HARDCOVER
EDITION OF THIS BOOK AS FOLLOWS:
Chödrön, Pema.
Taking the leap: freeing ourselves from old habits and fears /
Pema Chödrön; edited by Sandy Boucher.—1st ed.
p.   cm.
ISBN 978-1-59030-634-5 (hardcover)
ISBN 978-1-61180-683-0 (2019 paperback)
1. Spiritual life—Buddhism. I. Boucher, Sandy. II. Title.
BQ5670.C49 2009
294.3'444—dc22
2009010225

*This book is dedicated to the long life of both
His Holiness the 17th Karmapa Ugyen Trinley Dorje
and Venerable Dzigar Kongtrül Rinpoche*

CONTENTS

Feeding the Right Wolf   1

Learning to Stay   9

The Habit of Escape   15

The Natural Movement of Life   23

Getting Unstuck   27

We Have What We Need   35

Rejoicing in Things as They Are   43

Uncovering Natural Openness   49

The Importance of Pain   57

Unlimited Friendliness   65

Epilogue: Taking This into the World   73

Acknowledgments   75

Related Readings   77

Resources   79

About the Author   83

The Pema Chödrön Foundation   85

TAKING THE LEAP

ONE

FEEDING THE RIGHT WOLF

As human beings we have the potential to disentangle ourselves from old habits, and the potential to love and care about each other. We have the capacity to wake up and live consciously, but, you may have noticed, we also have a strong inclination to stay asleep. It's as if we are always at a crossroad, continuously choosing which way to go. Moment by moment we can choose to go toward further clarity and happiness or toward confusion and pain.

In order to make this choice skillfully, many of us turn to spiritual practices of various kinds with the wish that our lives will lighten up and that we'll find the strength to cope with our difficulties. Yet in these times it seems crucial that we also keep in mind the wider context in which we make choices about how to live: this is the context of our beloved earth and the rather rocky condition it's in.

For many, spiritual practice represents a way to relax and a way to access peace of mind. We want to feel more calm, more focused; and with our frantic and stressful lives, who can blame us? Nevertheless, we have a responsibility to think bigger than that these days. If spiritual practice is relaxing, if it gives us some peace of mind, that's great—but is this personal satisfaction helping us to address what's happening in the world? The main question is, are we living in a way that adds further aggression and self-centeredness to the mix, or are we adding some much-needed sanity?

Many of us feel deeply concerned about the state of the world. I know how sincerely people wish for things to change and for beings everywhere to be free of suffering. But if we're honest with ourselves, do we have any idea how to put this aspiration into practice when it comes to our own lives? Do we have any clarity about how our own words and actions may be causing suffering? And even if we do recognize that we're making a mess of things, do we have a clue about how to stop? These have always been important questions, but they are especially so today. This is a time when disentangling ourselves is about more than our personal happiness. Working on ourselves and becoming more conscious about our own minds and emotions may be the only way for us to find solutions that address the welfare of all beings and the survival of the earth itself.

There was a story that was widely circulated a few days after the attacks of September 11, 2001, that illustrates our dilemma. A Native American grandfather was speaking to his grandson about violence and cruelty in the world and how it comes about. He said it was as if two wolves were fighting in his heart. One wolf was vengeful and angry, and the other wolf was understanding and kind. The young man asked his grandfather which wolf would win the fight in his heart. And the grandfather answered, "The one that wins will be the one I choose to feed."

So this is our challenge, the challenge for our spiritual practice and the challenge for the world—how can we train right now, not later, in feeding the right wolf? How can we call on our innate intelligence to see what helps and what hurts, what escalates aggression and what uncovers our good-heartedness? With the global economy in chaos and the environment of the planet at risk, with war raging and suffering escalating, it is time for each of us in our own lives to take the leap and do whatever we can to help turn things around. Even the slightest gesture toward feeding the right wolf will help. Now more than ever, we are all in this together.

Taking the leap involves making a commitment to ourselves and to the earth itself—making a commitment to let go of old grudges, to not avoid people and situations and emotions that make us feel uneasy, to not cling to our fears, our closed-mindedness, our hard-heartedness, our hesitation. Now is the time to develop trust in our basic goodness and the basic goodness of our sisters and brothers on this earth; a time to develop confidence in our ability to drop our old ways of staying stuck and to choose wisely. We could do that right here and right now.

In our everyday encounters, we can live in a way that will help us learn to do this. When we talk to someone we don't like and don't agree with—maybe a family member or a person at work—we tend to spend a great amount of energy sending anger their way. Yet our resentments and self-centeredness, as familiar as they are, are not our basic nature. We all have the natural ability to interrupt old habits. All of us know how healing it is to be kind, how transformative it is to love, what a relief it is to have old grudges drop away. With just a slight shift in perspective, we can realize that people strike out and say mean things for the same reasons we do. With a sense of humor we can see that our sisters and brothers, our partners, our children, our coworkers are driving us crazy the same way we drive other people crazy.

The first step in this learning process is to be honest with ourselves. Most of us have gotten so good at empowering our negativity and insisting on our rightness that the angry wolf gets shinier and shinier, and the other wolf is just there with its pleading eyes. But we're not stuck with this way of being. When we're feeling resentment or any strong emotion, we can recognize that we are getting worked up, and realize that right now we can consciously make the choice to be aggressive or to cool off. It comes down to choosing which wolf we want to feed.

Of course, if we intend to test out this approach, we need some pointers. We need ways to train in this path of choosing wisely. This path entails uncovering three qualities of being human, three basic qualities that have always been with us but perhaps have gotten buried and been almost forgotten. These qualities are natural intelligence, natural warmth, and natural openness. When I say that the potential for goodness exists in all beings, that is acknowledging that everyone, everywhere, all over the globe, has these qualities and can call on them to help themselves and others.

Natural intelligence is always accessible to us. When we're not caught in the trap of hope and fear, we intuitively know what's the right thing to do. If we're not obscuring our intelligence with anger, self-pity, or craving, we know what will help and what will make things worse. Our well-perfected emotional reactions cause us to do and say a lot of crazy things. We desire to be happy and at peace, but when our emotions are aroused, somehow the methods we use to achieve this happiness only make us more miserable. Our wishes and our actions are, all too frequently, not in synch. Nevertheless, we all have access to a fundamental intelligence that can help to solve our problems rather than making them worse.

Natural warmth is our shared capacity to love, to have empathy, to have a sense of humor. It is also our capacity to feel gratitude and appreciation and tenderness. It's the whole gamut of what often are called the heart qualities, qualities that are a natural part of being human. Natural warmth has the power to heal all relationships—the relationship with ourselves as well as with people, animals, and all that we encounter every day of our lives.

The third quality of basic goodness is natural openness, the spaciousness of our skylike minds. Fundamentally, our minds are expansive, flexible, and curious; they are pre-prejudice, so to speak. This is the condition of mind before we narrow down into a fear-based view where everyone is either an enemy or a friend, a threat or an ally, someone to like, dislike, or ignore. Fundamentally, this mind that we have, that you and I each have, is open.

We can connect with that openness at any time. For instance, right now, for three seconds, just stop reading and pause.

If you were able to stop briefly like that, perhaps you experienced a thought-free moment.

Another way to appreciate natural openness is to think of a

time when you were angry, when someone said or did something that you didn't like, a time when you wanted to get even or you wanted to vent. Now, what if you had been able to stop, breathe deeply, and slow the process down? Right on the spot you could connect with natural openness. You could stop, give space, and empower the wolf of patience and courage instead of the wolf of aggression and violence. In that moment when we pause, our natural intelligence often comes to our rescue. We have time to reflect: why *do* we want to make that nasty phone call, say that mean word, or for that matter, drink the drink or smoke the substance or whatever it might be?

It's undeniable that we want to do these things because in that heated state we believe it will bring us some relief. Some kind of satisfaction or resolution or comfort will result: we think we'll feel better at the end. But what if we paused, and asked ourselves, "*Will* I feel better when this is over?" Allowing that openness, that space, gives our natural intelligence a chance to tell us what we already know: that we *won't* feel better at the end. And how do we know this? Because, believe it or not, this is not the first time we've gotten caught in the same impulse, the same automatic-pilot strategy. If we were to do a poll, probably most people would say that in their personal lives aggression breeds aggression. It escalates anger and ill will rather than bringing peace.

If right now our emotional reaction to seeing a certain person or hearing certain news is to fly into a rage or to get despondent or something equally extreme, it's because we have been cultivating that particular habit for a very long time. But as my teacher Chögyam Trungpa Rinpoche used to say, we can approach our lives as an experiment. In the next moment, in the next hour, we could choose to stop, to slow down, to be still for a few seconds. We could experiment with interrupting the usual chain reaction, and not spin off in the usual way. We don't need to blame someone else, and we don't need to blame ourselves. When we're in a tight spot, we can experiment with not strengthening the aggression habit and see what happens.

Pausing is very helpful in this process. It creates a momentary contrast between being completely self-absorbed and being awake and present. You just stop for a few seconds, breathe deeply, and move on. You don't want to make it into a project. Chögyam Trungpa used to refer to this as the gap. You pause and allow there to be a gap in whatever you're doing. The Vietnamese Buddhist master Thich Nhat Hanh teaches this as a mindfulness practice. At his monastery and retreat centers, at intervals someone rings a bell, and at the sound everyone stops briefly to breathe deeply and mindfully. In the middle of just living, which is usually a pretty caught-up experience characterized by a lot of internal discussion with yourself, you just pause.

Throughout the day, you could choose to do this. It may be hard to remember at first, but once you start doing it, pausing becomes something that nurtures you; you begin to prefer it to being all caught up.

People who have found this helpful create ways of interjecting pausing into their busy lives. For instance, they'll put a sign on their computer. It could be a word, or a face, an image, a symbol—anything that reminds them. Or they'll decide, "Every time the phone rings, I'm going to pause." Or "When I go to open my computer, I'm going to pause." Or "When I open the refrigerator, or wait in line, or brush my teeth . . . ." You can come up with anything that happens often during your day. You'll just be doing whatever you're doing, and then, for a few seconds, you pause and take three conscious breaths.

Some people have told me that they find it unnerving to pause. One man said if he pauses it feels like death to him. This speaks to the power of habit. We associate acting habitually with security, ground, and comfort. It gives us the feeling of something to hold on to. Our habit is just to keep moving, speeding, talking to ourselves, and filling up the space. But habits are like clothes. We can put them on and we can take them off. Yet, as we well know, when we get very attached to wearing clothes, we don't want to take them off. We feel as if we'll be too exposed, naked in front of everyone; we'll feel groundless and insecure and we won't know what's going on.

We think it's natural, even sane, to run away from those kinds of uncomfortable feelings. If you decide, quite enthusiastically, that every time you open your computer, you're going to pause, then when you actually open your computer, you may have an objection: "Well, *now* I can't pause because I'm in a rush and there are forty million things to do." We think this inability or this reluctance to slow down has something to do with our outer circumstances, because we live such busy lives. But I can tell you that I discovered otherwise when I was on a three-year retreat. I would be sitting in my small room looking out at the ocean, with all the time in the world. I would be silently meditating, and this queasy feeling would come over me; I'd feel that I just had to rush through my session so I could do something more important. When I experienced that, I realized that for all of us this is a *very* entrenched habit. The feeling is, quite simply, not wanting to be fully present.

In highly charged situations, or anytime at all, we could shake up our ancient fear-based habits by simply pausing. When we do that, we allow some space to contact the natural openness of our mind and let our natural intelligence emerge. Natural intelligence knows intuitively what will soothe and what will get us more churned up; this can be lifesaving information.

When we pause, we also give ourselves the chance to touch in to our natural warmth. When the heart qualities are awakened, they cut through our negativity in a way that nothing else can. A serviceman in Iraq told this story: He said it happened on a pretty typical day, when he had once again witnessed his fellow soldiers, people he loved, being blown up. And once again he and all the others in his division wanted revenge. When they located some Iraqi men who were possibly responsible for killing their friends, they went into the men's darkened house, and because of their anger and being in such a claustrophobic situation where violence was the atmosphere they breathed, the soldiers acted out their frustration by beating up the men.

Then when they put a flashlight on their captives' faces, they saw that one of them was only a young boy who had Down's syndrome.

This American serviceman had a son with Down's syndrome. When he saw the boy, it broke his heart, and suddenly he viewed the situation differently. He felt the boy's fear, and he saw that the Iraqis were human beings just like himself. His good heart was strong enough to cut through his pent-up rage, and he couldn't continue to brutalize them anymore. In a moment of natural compassion, his view of the war and what he'd been doing just shifted.

Currently, the majority of the world's population is far from being able to acknowledge when they're about to explode or even to think it's important to slow the process down. In most cases, that churned-up energy translates quickly into aggressive reactions and speech. Yet, for each and every one of us, intelligence, warmth, and openness are always accessible. If we can be conscious enough to realize what's happening, we can pause and uncover these basic human qualities. The wish for revenge, the prejudiced mind—all of that is temporary and removable. It's not the permanent state. As Chögyam Trungpa put it, "Sanity is permanent, neurosis is temporary."

To honestly face the pain in our lives and the problems in the world, let's start by looking compassionately and honestly at our own minds. We can become intimate with the mind of hatred, the mind that polarizes, the mind that makes somebody "other" and bad and wrong. We come to know, unflinchingly, and with great kindness, the angry, unforgiving, hostile wolf. Over time, that part of ourselves becomes very familiar, but we no longer feed it. Instead, we can make the choice to nurture openness, intelligence, and warmth. This choice, and the attitudes and actions that follow from it, are like a medicine that has the potential to cure all suffering.

TWO

LEARNING TO STAY

THE PRIMARY FOCUS OF THIS PATH OF CHOOSING WISELY, of this training to de-escalate aggression, is learning to stay present. Pausing very briefly, frequently throughout the day, is an almost effortless way to do this. For just a few seconds we can be right here. Meditation is another way to train in learning to stay, or, as one student put it more accurately, learning to come back, to return to being present over and over again. The truth is, anyone who's ever tried meditation learns really quickly that we are almost never fully present. I remember when I was first given meditation instruction. It sounds so simple: Just sit down, get comfortable, and bring light awareness to your breath. When your mind wanders, gently come back and stay present with your breath. I thought, "This will be easy." Then someone hit a gong to begin and I tried it. What I found was that I wasn't present with a single breath until they hit the gong again to end the session. I had spent the whole time lost in thought.

Back then I believed this was because of some failing of mine, and that if I stuck with meditation, soon I'd be perfect at it, attending to each and every breath. Maybe occasionally I'd be distracted by something, but mostly I would just stay present. Now it's about thirty years later. Sometimes my mind is busy. Sometimes it's still. Sometimes the energy is agitated. Sometimes calm. All kinds of things happen when we meditate—everything from thoughts to shortness of breath to visual images, from physical discomfort to mental distress to peak experiences. All of that happens, and the basic attitude is, "No big deal." The key point is that, through it all, we train in being open and receptive to whatever arises.

What I've noticed about the people whom I consider to be awake is this: They're fully conscious of whatever is happening. Their minds don't go off anywhere. They just stay right here with chaos, with silence, with a carnival, in an emergency room, on a mountainside: they're completely receptive and open to what's happening. It's at the same time the simplest and the most profound thing—rather like one continual pause.

But for sure we need tremendous encouragement and some practical advice for how to stay right here and open ourselves to life. It's definitely not our habitual response. My Buddhist teachers Chögyam Trungpa and Dzigar Kongtrül Rinpoche both used a helpful analogy to describe the challenge of staying present to life's discomfort. They said that we humans are like young children who have a bad case of poison ivy. Because we want to relieve the discomfort, we automatically scratch, and it seems a perfectly sane thing to do. In the face of anything we don't like, we automatically try to escape. In other words, scratching is our habitual way of trying to get away, trying to escape our fundamental discomfort, the fundamental itch of restlessness and insecurity, or that very uneasy feeling: that feeling that something bad is about to happen.

We don't know yet that when we scratch, the poison ivy spreads. Pretty soon we're scratching all over our body and rather than finding relief, we find that our discomfort is escalating.

In this analogy, the child is taken to the doctor to be given a prescription. This is equivalent to meeting a spiritual guide, receiving teachings, and beginning the practice of meditation. Meditation can be described as learning how to stay with the itch and the urge to scratch without scratching. With meditation we train in settling down with whatever we're feeling, including the addictive urge to scratch, the addictive urge to avoid discomfort at any cost. We train in just staying present, open, and awake, no matter what's going on.

Left to our own devices, however, we'll scratch forever, seeking the relief we never find. But the doctor gives us wise advice: "You have a bad case of poison ivy. It's definitely curable, but you'll have to follow some straightforward instructions. If you keep scratching, the itch will get much worse. That's for sure. So, apply this medicine, and it will help you to stop. In this way your misery will start to lessen and eventually cease." If the child has enough love for himself or herself and wants to heal, that unhappy child will follow the doctor's instructions. He or she will see the obvious logic of the doctor's words and go through the short-term discomfort of feeling an itch without scratching. And then, gradually, the child will reap the benefit. It isn't the doctor or anyone else who gets rewarded: it's you as you find that the rash starts to get better and the urge to scratch gradually goes away.

As many of us know, particularly those of us who have had strong addictions, it can take a very long time to learn to be with the itch. Nevertheless, it's the only way. If we keep scratching, not only does the itch get worse but we find ourselves more and more in hell. Our lives become more out of control and uncomfortable. The three classic styles of looking for relief in the wrong places are pleasure seeking, numbing out, and using aggression: we either zone out, or we grasp. Or perhaps we develop the style of scratching in which we obsess and rage about other people or indulge in self-hatred.

In the Buddhist teachings, it is said that the root of our discontent is self-absorption and our fear of being present. We can easily go from being open and receptive—an alive, awake feeling—to withdrawing. Again and again, we run from discomfort and go for short-term symptom relief, which never addresses the root of the problem. We're like an ostrich sticking its head in the sand in hopes of finding comfort. This running away from all that is unpleasant, this continual cycle of avoiding the present, is referred to as self-absorption, self-clinging, or ego.

One of the metaphors for ego is a cocoon. We stay in our cocoon because we're afraid—we're afraid of our feelings and the reactions that life is going to trigger in us. We're afraid of what might come at us. But if this avoidance strategy worked, then the Buddha wouldn't have needed to teach anything, because our attempts to escape pain, which all living beings instinctively resort to, would result in security, happiness, and comfort, and there would be no problem. But what the Buddha observed is that self-absorption, this trying to find zones of safety, creates terrible suffering. It weakens us, the world becomes more terrifying, and our thoughts and emotions become more and more threatening as well.

There are many ways to discuss ego, but in essence it's what I've been talking about. It's the experience of never being present. There is a deep-seated tendency, it's almost a compulsion, to distract ourselves, even when we're not consciously feeling uncomfortable. Everybody feels a little bit of an itch all the time. There's a background hum of edginess, boredom, restlessness. As I've said, during my time in retreat where there were almost no distractions, even there I experienced this deep uneasiness.

The Buddhist explanation is that we feel this uneasiness because we're always trying to get ground under our feet and it never quite works. We're always looking for a permanent reference point, and it doesn't exist. Everything is impermanent. Everything is always changing—fluid, unfixed, and open. Nothing is pin-down-able the way we'd like it to be. This is not actually bad news, but we all seem to be programmed for denial. We have absolutely no tolerance for uncertainty.

It seems that insecurity is ego's reaction to the shifting nature of reality. We tend to find the groundlessness of our fundamental situation extremely uncomfortable. Virtually everybody knows this basic insecurity, and often we experience it as horrible. With me in that same three-year retreat was a woman with whom I'd once been close friends. Something had happened between us, though, and I felt now that she hated me. We were in a very small building together, we had to pass each other in the narrow corridors, and there was no way to get away from each other. She was very angry and wouldn't talk to me, and that brought up feelings of profound helplessness. My usual strategies were not working. I was continually feeling the pain of no reference point, no confirmation. The ways I had always used to feel secure and in control had fallen apart. I tried all the techniques I had been teaching for years, but nothing really worked.

So one night, since I couldn't sleep, I went up to the meditation hall, and sat all through the night. I was just sitting with raw pain with almost no thoughts about it. Then something happened: I had a completely clear insight that my whole personality, my whole ego-structure, was based on not wanting to go to this ground-less place. Everything I did, the way I smiled, the way I talked to people, the way I tried to please everybody—it was all to avoid feeling this way. I realized that our whole façade, the little song and dance we all do, is based on trying to avoid the groundless-ness that permeates our lives.

By learning to stay, we become very familiar with this place, and gradually, gradually, it loses its threat. Instead of scratching, we stay present. We're no longer invested in constantly trying to move away from insecurity. We think that facing our demons is reliving some traumatic event or discovering for sure that we're worthless. But, in fact, it is just abiding with the uneasy, disquieting sensation of nowhere-to-run and finding that—guess what?—we don't die; we don't collapse. In fact, we feel profound relief and freedom.

One way to practice staying present is to pause, look out, and take three deep breaths. Another way is to simply sit still for a while and listen. Simply listen to the sounds in the room. For one minute, listen to the sounds close to you. For one minute, listen to the sounds at a distance. Just listen attentively. The sound isn't good or bad. It's just sound.

Maybe in that experience of listening you found that you have the capacity for attention. The capacity to be present with alert-ness. On the other hand, your mind may have wandered off. When that happens—whether the object of meditation is the breath, a sound, a sensation, or a feeling—when you notice that your mind has wandered off, you gently come back. You come back because the present is so precious and fleeting, and because without some reference point to come back to, we never notice that we're distracted—that once again we're looking for an alternative to being fully present, an alternative to being here with things just exactly as they are rather than the way we would prefer them to be.

THREE

THE HABIT OF ESCAPE

I T SEEMS WE ALL HAVE THE TENDENCY TO MOVE AWAY from the present moment. It's as if this habit is built into our DNA. At the most basic level, we think all the time and this takes us away. In his teachings on the difference between fantasy and reality, Chögyam Trungpa said that being fully present, having contact with the immediacy of our experience, is reality. Fantasy he described as being lost in thought. All those people driving on the freeway at 85 miles per hour: most of them are distracted. Apparently we have some kind of automatic pilot that keeps us on the road, or keeps us multitasking, or eating, or all the other things we do quite mindlessly. This pattern of distracting ourselves, of not being fully present, of not contacting the immediacy of our experience is considered normal.

From a Buddhist perspective, lifetime after lifetime we've been strengthening this habit of distraction. If you don't buy the idea of rebirth, just this lifetime is enough to see how we do it. Since we were children, we've strengthened the habit of escape, choosing fantasy over reality. Unfortunately, we get a lot of comfort from leaving, from being lost in our thoughts, worries, and plans. It gives us a sense of false security and we enjoy it.

There's a very useful teaching, which I heard from Dzigar Kongtrül, that allows us to take a closer look at this knee-jerk pattern of moving away from being present. This is the teaching on *shenpa*. Generally the Tibetan word *shenpa* is translated "attachment," but that has always seemed too abstract to me, as it doesn't touch the magnitude of shenpa and the effect it has on us.

An alternate translation might be "hooked"—what it feels like to get hooked—what it feels like to be stuck. Everyone likes to hear teachings on getting unstuck because they address such a common source of pain. In terms of the poison-ivy metaphor—our fundamental itch and the habit of scratching—shenpa is the itch and it's also the urge to scratch. The urge to smoke that cigarette, the urge to overeat, to have one more drink, to say something cruel or to tell a lie.

Here's how shenpa shows up in everyday experiences. Somebody says a harsh word and something in you tightens: instantly you're hooked. That tightness quickly spirals into blaming the person or denigrating yourself. The chain reaction of speaking or acting or obsessing happens fast. Maybe, if you have strong addictions, you go right for your addiction to cover over the uncomfortable feelings. This is very personal. What was said gets to you—it triggers you. It might not bother someone else at all, but we're talking about what touches your sore place—that sore place of shenpa.

The fundamental, most basic shenpa is to ego itself: attachment to our identity, the image of who we think we are. When we experience our identity as being threatened, our self-absorption gets very strong, and shenpa automatically arises. Then there is the spin-off—such as attachment to our possessions or to our views and opinions. For example, someone criticizes you. They criticize your politics, they criticize your appearance, they criticize your dearest friend. And shenpa is right there. As soon as the words have registered—boom, it's there. Shenpa is not the thoughts or emotions per se. Shenpa is preverbal, but it breeds thoughts and emotions very quickly. If we're attentive, we can feel it happening.

If we catch it when it first arises, when it's just a tightening, a slight pulling back, a feeling of beginning to get hot under the collar, it's very workable. Then we have the possibility of becoming curious about this urge to do the habitual thing, this urge to strengthen a repetitive pattern. We can feel it physically and, interestingly enough, it's never new. It always has a familiar taste. It has a familiar smell. When you begin to get in touch with shenpa, you feel like this has been happening forever. It allows you to feel the underlying insecurity that is inherent in a changing, shifting, impermanent world—an insecurity that is felt by everyone as long as we continue to scramble to get ground under our feet.

When someone says something that triggers you, you don't really have to go into the history of why you're triggered. This is not self-analysis, an exploration of what the trauma was. It's just, "Uh-oh," and you feel yourself tightening. Generally speaking, we don't catch it when it first arises. It's more common to be well into acting out or repressing by the time we realize that we're caught.

Dzigar Kongtrül says that shenpa is the charge behind emotions, behind thoughts and words. For instance, when words are imbued with shenpa, they easily become hate words. Any word at all can be transformed into a racial slur, into the language of aggression, when it has the force and charge of shenpa behind it. You say the shenpa word and it produces shenpa in others, who then respond defensively. When left unchecked, shenpa is similar to a highly contagious disease and it spreads rapidly.

There's a word that is currently used to dehumanize people in the Middle East. I've heard that United States soldiers are taught it before they go there. The word is *haji*. One serviceman told me it's common to hear, "It's OK, they're just haji," as a justification for mistreating or killing innocent civilians. The poignant thing is that in Islamic culture the word has a very positive connotation. It is the honorific term for one who has made the pilgrimage to the sacred site of Mecca. So words themselves are neutral, it's the charge we add to them that matters. When there's shenpa, the word *haji* dehumanizes people. It becomes the language of hatred and violence. Without that charge, without that heat, the same word produces completely different reactions in the hearts and minds of those who hear it.

We all use shenpa words. We may try never to use those that are outright racial slurs, but we have our ways of deriding others.

When you don't like someone, even their name can become a shenpa word. For instance, when you speak of your lifelong rival, Jane, or your brother, Bill, whom you loathe, the very tone of voice with which you say their name conveys disdain and aggression.

You can notice shenpa very easily in other people. You're having a conversation with somebody and they are right with you, listening. Then, after something you say, you see them tense. Somehow you know you just touched a sensitive area. You're seeing their shenpa, but they may not be aware of it at all.

When we see clearly what's happening to another person, we have access to our natural intelligence. We know instinctively that the important thing we are trying to communicate will not get through right now. The person is shutting down, he or she is closing off because of shenpa. Our natural wisdom tells us to be quiet and not push our point; we intuitively know that no one will win if we spread the virus of shenpa.

Whenever there's discomfort or restlessness or boredom—whenever there's insecurity in any form—shenpa clicks in. This is true for us all. If we become familiar with it, we can fully experience that unease. We can fully experience the shenpa and learn over time that it's in everyone's best interest not to act it out.

Not acting out, or refraining, is very interesting. It's also called renunciation in the Buddhist teachings. The Tibetan word for renunciation is *shenluk,* and it means turning shenpa upside down, shaking it up completely. It means getting unhooked. Renunciation isn't about renouncing food, or sex, or your lifestyle. We're not referring to giving up the things themselves. We're talking about loosening our attachment, the shenpa we have to these things.

In general, Buddhism encourages us never to reject what is problematic but rather to become very familiar with it. And so it is here: we are urged to acknowledge our shenpa, see it clearly, experience it fully—without acting out or repressing.

If we are willing to acknowledge our shenpa and to experience it without sidetracks, then our natural intelligence begins to guide us. We begin to foresee the whole chain reaction and where it will lead. There's some wisdom that becomes accessible to us—wisdom based on compassion for oneself and others that has nothing to do with ego's fears. It's the part of us that knows we can connect and live from our basic goodness, our basic intelligence, openness, and warmth. Over time, this knowledge becomes a stronger force than the shenpa, and we naturally interrupt the chain reaction before it even starts. We naturally become able to prevent an epidemic of aggression before it even begins.

In my own training, I have always been instructed not to get caught up in accepting and rejecting, not to get caught by biased mind. Chögyam Trungpa was particularly emphatic about this. At one time, this presented a question for me: Did it mean I should not have preferences such as liking one kind of flower or one kind of food far better than another? Was it problematic not to like the taste of raw onions or the smell of patchouli oil? Or to feel more at home with Buddhism than with another philosophy or religion?

When I heard the teaching on shenpa, my dilemma was resolved. The issue isn't with preferences but with the shenpa behind them. If I get worked up when presented with raw onions, if the very sight of them triggers aversion in me, then the bias is deep. I'm clearly hooked. If I start an anti-raw-onion campaign or write an anti-patchouli-oil book or begin to attack another philosophy or religion, then it's shenpa, big time. My mind and heart are closed. I'm so invested in my views and opinions that those who think differently are my adversaries. I become a fundamentalist: one who feels strongly that I am right and who closes my mind to those who think otherwise. On the other hand, Martin Luther King, Jr., and Gandhi are both examples of how we can take a stand and speak out without shenpa. As they demonstrated, being without shenpa does not lead to complacency, it leads to open-mindedness and compassionate action.

Of course, we get hooked by positive experiences as well as negative experiences. When we really want something, shenpa is usually there. This becomes a fairly common experience for meditators. You meditated and you felt a settling, a calmness, a sense of well-being. Maybe thoughts came and went, but they didn't seduce you, and you were able to come back to the present. There wasn't a sense of struggle. So, ironically, then you get attached to your success. "I did it right, I got it right, that's how it should always be. That's the model." But it wasn't "right" or "good," it was just what it was. Because of shenpa, you get hooked by positive experience.

Then the next time you meditate, you obsess about someone at home, some unfinished project at work, something delicious to eat. You worry and you fret, or you feel fear or craving, and when you try to rope in your wild-horse mind, it refuses to be tamed. At the end you feel like it was a horrible meditation and you condemn yourself because you've failed. But it wasn't "bad." It was just what it was. Because of shenpa, you get attached to a self-image of failure. That's where it gets sticky.

The sad part is that all we're trying to do is not feel that underlying uneasiness. The sadder part is that we proceed in such a way that the uneasiness only gets worse. The message here is that the only way to ease our pain is to experience it fully. Learn to stay. Learn to stay with uneasiness, learn to stay with the tightening, learn to stay with the itch and urge of shenpa, so that the habitual chain reaction doesn't continue to rule our lives, and the patterns that we consider unhelpful don't keep getting stronger as the days and months and years go by. Someone once sent me a bone-shaped dog tag that you could wear on a cord around your neck. Instead of a dog's name, it said, "Sit. Stay. Heal." We can heal ourselves and the world by training in this way.

Once you see what you do, how you get hooked, and how you get swept away, it's hard to be arrogant. This honest recognition softens you up, humbles you in the best sense. It also begins to give you confidence in your basic goodness. When we are not blinded by the intensity of our emotions, when we allow a bit of space, a chance for a gap, when we pause, we naturally know what to do. We begin, due to our own wisdom, to move toward letting go and fearlessness. Due to our own wisdom, we gradually stop strengthening habits that only bring more pain to the world.

FOUR

THE NATURAL MOVEMENT OF LIFE

W E ARE ALL A MIXTURE OF AGGRESSION AND LOVING-kindness, hard-heartedness and tender open-heartedness, small-mindedness and forgiving open mind. We are not a fixed, predictable, static identity that anyone can point to and say, "You are always like this. You are always the same."

Life's energy is never static. It is as shifting, fluid, changing as the weather. Sometimes we like how we're feeling, sometimes we don't. Then we like it again. Then we don't. Happy and sad, comfortable and uncomfortable alternate continually. This is how it is for everyone.

But behind our views and opinions, our hopes and fears about what's happening, the dynamic energy of life is always here, un-changed by our reactions of like and dislike.

How we relate to this dynamic flow of energy is important. We can learn to relax with it, recognizing it as our basic ground, as a natural part of life; or the feeling of uncertainty, of nothing to hold on to, can cause us to panic, and instantly a chain reaction begins. We panic, we get hooked, and then our habits take over and we think and speak and act in a very predictable way.

Our energy and the energy of the universe are always in flux, but we have little tolerance for this unpredictability, and we have little ability to see ourselves and the world as an exciting, fluid situation that is always fresh and new. Instead we get stuck in a rut—the rut of "I want" and "I don't want," the rut of shenpa, the rut of continually getting hooked by our personal preferences.

The source of our unease is the unfulfillable longing for a lasting certainty and security, for something solid to hold on to. Unconsciously we expect that if we could just get the right job, the right partner, the right *something*, our lives would run smoothly. When anything unexpected or not to our liking happens, we think something has gone wrong. I believe this is not an exaggeration of where we find ourselves. Even at the most mundane level, we get so easily triggered—someone cuts in front of us, we get seasonal allergies, our favorite restaurant is closed when we arrive for dinner. We are never encouraged to experience the ebb and flow of our moods, of our health, of the weather, of outer events—pleasant and unpleasant—in their fullness. Instead we stay caught in a fearful, narrow holding pattern of avoiding any pain and continually seeking comfort. This is the universal dilemma.

When we pause, allow a gap, and breathe deeply, we can experience instant refreshment. Suddenly we slow down, look out, and there's the world. It can feel like briefly standing in the eye of the tornado or the still point of a turning wheel. Our mood may be agitated or cheerful. What we see and hear may be chaos or it may be the ocean, the mountains, or birds flying across a clear blue sky. Either way, momentarily our mind is still and we are not pulled in or pushed away by what we are experiencing.

Or we may experience this pause as awkward, as fearful, as impatient, as embarrassingly self-conscious.

The approach here is radical. We are encouraged to get comfortable with, begin to relax with, lean in to, *whatever* the experience may be. We are encouraged to drop the storyline and simply pause, look out, and breathe. Simply be present for a few seconds, a few minutes, a few hours, a whole lifetime, with our own shifting energies and with the unpredictability of life as it unfolds, wholly partaking in all experiences just exactly as they are.

On this journey of awakening, this journey of learning to be present, it is very helpful to recognize shenpa when it's happening. It may be subtle, just a slight pulling back, an involuntary tightening, or it may be full blown and highly charged. It doesn't matter, really, whether you catch shenpa as an ember or as a raging forest fire. If you can take the first step and acknowledge you're hooked—that already is interrupting an ancient habitual response. That already is interrupting the momentum, even if very briefly, of going on automatic pilot and exiting. You're wide awake, conscious that you're hooked and that right now you have a choice: you can empower shenpa or you can do something different. It's a highly charged moment in which you can escalate the intensity further or you can choose to pause and experience the uncomfortable energy without struggling.

Instead of seeing shenpa as an obstacle to be overcome, it is more helpful to consider it an opportunity for transformation, an open doorway to awakening. When I realize I'm triggered, I think of it as a neutral moment, a moment in time, a moment of truth that can go either way. What I'm advocating is that in that precious moment we start to make choices that lead to happiness and freedom rather than choices that lead to unnecessary suffering and the obscuration of our intelligence, our warmth, our capacity to remain open and present with the natural movement of life.

Ulysses, the hero of ancient Greek mythology, exemplifies the courage it takes to consciously choose staying receptive and present when the temptation to get swept away is intense. When he was making the sea voyage home to Greece after the Trojan War, Ulysses knew that his ship would have to pass through a very dangerous area that was inhabited by beautiful maidens known as the sirens. He had been warned that the call of these women was irresistible, and that sailors couldn't help but steer toward the sirens, crash their boats onto the rocks, and drown. Nevertheless, Ulysses wanted to hear the song of the sirens. He knew the prediction that if anyone could hear their voices and not go toward them, the sirens would lose their power forever and wither away. This was a challenge that drew him.

As his ship neared the sirens' homeland, Ulysses told his men to put wax plugs in their ears and to tie him tightly to the mast, instructing them that no matter how hard he struggled and gestured, no matter how wrathfully he appeared to be ordering them to cut his ropes, they were not to untie him until the ship reached a familiar point of land well out of earshot of the sirens' song. This story, as you might expect, has a happy ending. The men followed his instructions and Ulysses made it through. To a greater or lesser degree we will all have to go through similar discomfort in order not to follow the call of our own personal sirens, in order to step through the open doorway to awakening.

Each of us can be an active participant in creating a nonviolent future simply by how we work with shenpa when it arises. How individuals like you and I relate to being hooked, these days, has global implications. In that neutral moment, that often highly charged moment, when we can go either way, do we consciously strengthen old fear-based habits, or do we stay on the dot, fully experiencing the agitated, restless energy and letting it naturally unwind and flow on? There will be no lack of opportunities and no lack of material to work with.

Looking closely at this process, as I have for some years, it's easy to see that it takes courage to simply relax with our own dynamic energy, just as it is, without splitting off and trying to escape. It takes the courage, determination, and curiosity of a Ulysses to stay open and receptive to the energy of shenpa—to the itch and urge of shenpa—and not scratch in a habitual way.

FIVE

GETTING UNSTUCK

T HERE ARE THREE THINGS THAT I'VE OBSERVED ABOUT shenpa. One, our storyline fuels it. Two, it comes with an undertow. And three, it always has consequences—which frequently are not pleasant. For instance, we feel lonely and automatically shenpa is there—that neutral moment of shenpa is right there. But instead of recognizing what's happening, instead of waking up and riding the energy, we bite the hook and overeat, go on a binge, or strike out at others aggressively. Then there's the post-shenpa shenpa. We become hooked by guilt and self-denigration for having been taken over once again. The story can go on and on for years, with one shenpa setting off a chain reaction that gives birth to further shenpa and so on and on.

In this process of exploring shenpa, I've understood that it is crucial to drop the storyline. It's the conversations we have with ourselves in that neutral moment when we acknowledge we're hooked that turn a slight feeling of unease, a vague tightening of our jaw or stomach, into unkind words, dismissive gestures, or even violence. But it will remain an ember and gradually die out, the energy will ebb and then it will naturally flow on, if we don't fuel it, if we don't freeze it, with our storylines.

In meditation we're instructed to acknowledge when we're thinking and then to let the thoughts go and come back to being fully present—back to what Chögyam Trungpa called square one. Just keep coming back to square one, and if square one feels edgy and restless and filled with shenpa, still you just come back there. The shenpa itself is not the problem. The ignorance that doesn't acknowledge that you're hooked, that just goes unconscious and allows you to act it out—*that's* the problem. To counteract it, we try to bring our full compassionate attention to being hooked and what follows—the familiar chain reaction. We train in letting the storyline go, letting the fuel of shenpa go.

This is hard to do because then for sure you're left in a very uncomfortable place. When you don't do the habitual thing, you're bound to feel some pain. I call it the detox period. You've been doing the same predictable thing to get away from that uneasy, uncomfortable, vulnerable feeling for so long, and now you're not. So you're left with that queasy feeling. This requires some getting used to and some ability to practice kindness and patience. It requires some openness and curiosity to see what happens next. What happens when you don't fuel the discomfort with a storyline? What happens when you abide with this shifting, fluid, universal energy? What happens if you pause and embrace the natural movement of life?

What you learn very quickly in this process is what happens when you *don't* abide with the energy. You learn, as I've said, that the storyline feeds the shenpa, that it comes with an undertow, and that there will be consequences.

The undertow can be very strong. As Dzigar Kongtrül says, one of the qualities of shenpa is that it's very difficult to let go of. The urge to get even, the power of craving, the potency of sheer habit is like a magnetic force pulling us in a familiar direction. So we opt again and again for short-term gratification that in the long run keeps us stuck in the same cycle. If you've done this enough—especially if you've gone through this cycle consciously—you know that the consequences are easily predictable.

When we pause and breathe and abide with the energy, we can foresee quite clearly where biting the hook will lead. Gradually this understanding, this natural intelligence, supports us in our journey of abiding with the restless energy, our journey of fully partaking in our experience without being seduced by the shenpa of "I like it" or "I can't bear to feel this." Dzigar Kongtrül once pointed out that you may find a particular feeling intolerable, but instead of acting on that you could come to know intolerableness very, very well. Shantideva, the eighth-century Buddhist master, compares this to willingly undergoing a painful medical treatment in order to cure a long-term disease.

There is a formal practice for learning to stay with the energy of uncomfortable emotions—a practice for transmuting the poison of negative emotions into wisdom. It is similar to alchemy, the medieval technique of changing base metal into gold. You don't get rid of the base metal—it isn't thrown out and replaced by gold. Instead, the crude metal itself is the source of the precious gold. An analogy that's commonly used by Tibetans is of the peacock who eats poison with the result that its tail feathers become more brilliant and glowing.

This transmutation practice is specifically one of remaining open and receptive to your own energy when you are triggered. It has three steps.

Step One. Acknowledge that you're hooked.

Step Two. Pause, take three conscious breaths, and lean in. Lean in to the energy. Abide with it. Experience it fully. Taste it. Touch it. Smell it. Get curious about it. How does it feel in your body? What thoughts does it give birth to? Become very intimate with the itch and urge of shenpa and keep breathing. Part of this step is learning not to be seduced by the momentum of shenpa. Like Ulysses, we can find our way to hear the call of the sirens without being seduced. It's a process of staying awake and compassionate, interrupting the momentum, and refraining from causing harm. Just do not speak, do not act, and feel the energy. Be one with your own energy, one with the ebb and flow of life. Rather than rejecting the energy, embrace it. This leaning in is very open, very curious and intelligent.

Step Three. Then relax and move on. Just go on with your life so that the practice doesn't become a big deal, an endurance test, a contest that you win or lose.

The biggest challenge in doing this practice is to embrace the restless energy, to stay awake to it rather than automatically exiting. When we first start experimenting with this, we find that we can abide with the unpleasantness and pull ourselves out of the tailspin for only brief moments, after which, automatically, habit takes over again.

My beloved seven-year-old grandson, Pete, is a great example of this. He frequently melts down about the unfairness of life. Pete has a wonderful open quality and a great sense of humor, but when he's having one of his meltdowns, he temporarily loses all his brilliance and lets the storyline take over, as in: "My younger brother gets everything and I never get anything." "The world is unfair and I'm a victim." Reasoning with him definitely doesn't help. He quickly starts crumbling and gets so worked up that he shakes with rage.

Pete was obsessed with the *Star Wars* series at that time, so one day when this was happening, I asked him, "Pete, what would Obi-Wan Kenobi do?" Pete got a curious, receptive look on his face. I could see him contemplating my question, and he began to sit up very straight and smile. He suddenly manifested as a powerful person who trusted in himself. But then he couldn't resist—he started the storyline again. It was all about how his brother got this, and his brother got that, he never got anything, and he began to crumble again. I took a chance and once more reminded him of Obi-Wan Kenobi. And very, very, very briefly he once again pulled himself up and connected with his innate nobility.

It's like this for all of us initially. We can contact our inner strength, our natural openness, for short periods before getting swept away. And this is excellent, heroic, a huge step in interrupting and weakening our ancient habits. If we keep a sense of humor and stay with it for the long haul, the ability to be present just naturally evolves. Gradually we lose our appetite for biting the hook. We lose our appetite for aggression.

If we choose to work with this kind of practice, it's wise to start by practicing with little bouts of shenpa, the small irritations that happen all the time. If we become familiar with catching ourselves, acknowledging that we're hooked, and pausing in these ordinary everyday situations, then when major upheavals come, the practice will be available to us automatically. If we think we can wait until a major crisis arrives and then it will spontaneously click in, we're wrong.

Traffic is a great place to work with shenpa. Consider the unreasonable amount of charge that arises around other people's driving habits, or someone taking the parking place you thought was yours. Instead of just mindlessly feeding the irritation, you can recognize this as a perfect opportunity to do the transmutation practice.

Acknowledge you're hooked (with humor, if possible).

Pause, take three conscious breaths, and lean in to the energy (with kindness, if possible).

Relax and move on.

The wisest approach is that we try out this practice. We try it out in our lives today, tomorrow, right now—as long as we're alive, we practice this way of living.

Sometimes the only way we learn is the hard way. We might acknowledge that we're hooked but go ahead and do what we always do anyway—but we can do this as a conscious experiment to see where it will lead. When we're conscious, it allows us to learn from our mistakes.

I have an example of how painful this can be. Once I was staying at my daughter's house and for some reason I was feeling raw and out of sorts. In that prickly mood I received an upsetting e-mail, and the shenpa, which was already percolating, kicked in with a vengeance. You have probably all had that e-mail or voice mail experience. It was Sunday night, so I decided to avoid talking directly to the woman who sent the e-mail by calling her work number and leaving an angry message. When she came into the office on Monday, she was going to get my call. I felt justified because I knew that I was in a position of power, that basically I was going to get what I wanted because this particular company needed my cooperation.

I let that storyline blind me and I thought, "I am just going to tell it like it is, I'm going to set her straight!" I cringe now when I think of some of the obnoxious, arrogant things I said, practically to the degree of "Do you know who you're talking to?"

Then I hung up the phone, and of course I was still in the throes of shenpa, convincing myself that I was right to have called and stubbornly fueling my righteous indignation. My daughter had been sitting there listening to the whole thing, and the look on her face, I'd never seen anything like it. She was absolutely flabbergasted, and what she said next I considered a great compliment since I was at the time sixty-eight years old and she was in her mid-forties. She said, "Mom, I have never seen you lose it like that." I thought that was pretty good. But still I let shenpa take over and kept justifying what I had done. Seeing my daughter's total astonishment at my outburst finally brought me to my senses. I thought to myself, "Hmmm, well, it's done. Let's see what happens next."

What happened was I *did* get exactly what I wanted—you could say, in worldly terms, that I won. But this woman could never see me in the same light again. To this day, she's very polite and businesslike, but something shifted in her heart because she had always seen me as a spiritual teacher and someone who had it together, and then she got a voice mail from this neurotic witch. It didn't do any good to say I'm sorry, which I definitely said. I said it for a year almost every time we talked, but there was no way to change what had happened. So I received a valuable lesson from that; sometimes we just have to learn the hard way.

Shantideva reminds us that by "putting up with little cares," with minor annoyances, when the shenpa is lightweight, "we train ourselves to work with great adversity." By putting up with learning to keep our nobility, to not spin off, to not reject our own energy when the challenge is fairly workable, we train for difficult times. This is how we prepare ourselves to work with any highly charged situations that may come our way in the near or distant future.

Of course, neither you nor I know what adversity might or might not be coming—either in our personal or collective experience. Things could get better or they could get worse. We could inherit a fortune, or we or those we love could get an incurable illness. We could move into the house we've always wanted, or the house we live in could burn down. We could experience perfect health, or overnight we could become disabled. And at the global level, things could improve or deteriorate. The condition of the natural environment and the economy could stabilize, or disasters might occur. We never know for certain where present conditions will lead or what will happen next. There is, however, no need to be a prophet of doom or for us to go around living in constant dread. Our situation is definitely workable. By learning not to bite the hook now, with the little annoyances of an ordinary day, we'll be preparing ourselves to work with *whatever* lies ahead with compassion and wisdom.

SIX

WE HAVE WHAT WE NEED

I N THE BUDDHIST TEACHINGS WE'RE ENCOURAGED TO
work with the wildness of our minds and emotions as the absolute best way to dissolve our confusion and pain. Rather than
getting so caught in the drama of who did what to whom, we could
simply recognize that we're all worked up and stop fueling our
emotions with our stories. It's not so easy to do, but it's the key
to our well-being. In meditation we train in letting our thoughts
go again and again, over and over, and go right to the root of our
discontent. We allow the space to see the very mechanics of how
we keep ourselves stuck.

The teachings on multiple lifetimes are interesting in this regard. In this lifetime, perhaps a particular person harmed us, and
it can be helpful to know that. But on the other hand, possibly
ours is a far more ancient wound; perhaps we've been carrying
these same tendencies, these same ways of reacting, from lifetime
to lifetime, and they keep giving birth to the same dramas, the
same predicaments.

Whether we allow for the possibility of rebirth or not, still this
kind of thinking can be helpful if it inspires us to put the emphasis
on seeing through our shenpa tendencies as they are manifesting right now rather than dwelling on our painful histories. No
matter what happened to us in the past, right now we can take
responsibility for working compassionately with our habits, our
thoughts and emotions. We can take the emphasis off who hurt
us and put it on disentangling ourselves. If someone shoots an

arrow into my chest, I can let the arrow fester while I scream at my attacker, or I can remove the arrow as quickly as possible. In this very lifetime, I have what it takes to change the movie of my life so that the same things don't keep happening to me. It does seem that the same things keep coming back to trigger the same feelings in us until we've made friends with them. Our attitude can be that we keep getting another chance, rather than that we're just getting another bad deal.

For just a moment or two, pause and contact whatever you are feeling right now. If you can precede this by recollecting something that's bothering you, that will be even more helpful. If you can contact feelings such as worry, hopelessness, impatience, resentment, righteous indignation, or craving, that will be especially rewarding.

For a moment or more, touch the quality, the mood, the bodily felt sensation free of the storyline. This uncomfortable experience, this familiar sensation that can sit like a lump in your stomach, that can cause your body and face to tense, that can physically hurt—this experience itself is not a problem. If we can get curious about this emotional reaction, if we can relax and feel it, if we can experience it fully and let it be, then it's no problem. We might even experience it as simply frozen energy whose true nature is fluid, dynamic, and creative—just an ungraspable sensation free of our interpretation.

Our repetitive suffering does not come from this uncomfortable sensation but from what happens next, what I've been calling following the momentum, spinning off, or getting swept away. It comes from rejecting our own energy when it comes in a form we don't like. It comes from continually strengthening habits of grasping and aversion and distancing ourselves. In particular it comes from our internal conversations—our judgments, embellishments, and labels about what's happening.

But if we choose to practice by acknowledging, pausing, abiding with the energy, and then moving on, the power of this is not just that it weakens old habits but that it burns up the propensity for these habits altogether. The truly wonderful aspect of living this way is that it leaves the space wide open for a completely fresh experience free of self-absorption. Right here, exactly where we are, we can live from a broader perspective, one that admits all experiences—pleasurable, painful, and neutral. We are free to appreciate the infinite possibilities that are always available, free to recognize the natural openness, intelligence, and warmth of the human mind.

If the teachings on shenpa resonate with us, and we start practicing with them in our meditation and in our daily life, then very likely we'll begin to ask some truly useful questions. Instead of asking, How can I get rid of my difficult coworker, or how can I get even with my abusive father, we might begin to wonder how to unwind our suffering at the root. We might wonder, How do I learn to recognize I'm caught? How can I see what I do without feeling hopeless? How can I find some sense of humor? Some gentleness? Some ability to let go and not make such a big deal of my problems? What will help me remain present when I'm afraid?

We might also ask, Given my present situation, how long should I stay with uncomfortable feelings? This is a good question, yet there is no right answer. We simply get accustomed to coming back to the present just as it is for a second, for a minute, for an hour—whatever is currently natural—without its becoming an endurance trial. Just pausing for two to three breaths is a perfect way to stay present. This is a good use of our life. Indeed, it is an excellent, joyful use of our life. Instead of getting better and better at avoiding, we can learn to accept the present moment as if we had invited it, and work with it instead of against it, making it our ally rather than our enemy.

This is a work in progress, a process of uncovering our natural openness, uncovering our natural intelligence and warmth. I have discovered, just as my teachers always told me, that we already have what we need. The wisdom, the strength, the confidence, the awakened heart and mind are always accessible, here, now, always. We are just uncovering them. We are rediscovering them.

We're not inventing them or importing them from somewhere else. They're here. That's why when we feel caught in darkness, suddenly the clouds can part. Out of nowhere we cheer up or relax or experience the vastness of our minds. No one else gives this to you. People will support you and help you with teachings and practices, as they have supported and helped me, but you yourself experience your unlimited potential.

In my case, I'm trained in a tradition and a lineage where devotion to our teachers is an important way of connecting with openness and warmth. Their very presence can cause the clouds to part. I feel that my teachers would do anything to help me, just as their teachers helped them. However, we're taught never to depend on the teacher. The teacher's role is to wean us from leaning on him or her, to wean us from dependency altogether, and to help us finally grow up.

It's a matter of wisdom resonating with wisdom, of our wisdom resonating with the teacher's. If we apply their teachings to our lives and practice what they teach, we can realize what they have realized. Our devotion to a teacher has nothing to do with his or her lifestyle or worldly accomplishments. It's their state of mind, the quality of their heart that we resonate with. When it comes to my teacher Chögyam Trungpa, he was so outrageous in his behavior that I could never model myself after him. But I do try to model myself on his way of being. He showed me by his example that we can rouse ourselves fearlessly and encourage one another to be sane.

There is certainly no one easy answer for how to be free of suffering, but our teachers do all they can to guide us by giving us a sort of spiritual toolbox. The toolbox contains relative, usable teachings and practices, as well as an introduction to the absolute view of reality: that neither thoughts, emotions, nor shenpa are as solid as they appear. The main tool, and one that embodies both the relative and the absolute, is the practice of sitting meditation, especially as it was taught by Chögyam Trungpa. He described the basic practice as being completely present. And emphasized that it allowed the space for our neuroses to come to the surface. It was not, as he put it, "a vacation from irritation."

He stressed that this basic practice, which is epitomized by the instruction to return again and again to the immediacy of our experience, to the breath, the feeling, or other object of meditation, uncovers a complete openness to things just as they are without conceptual padding. It allows us to lighten up and to appreciate our world and ourselves unconditionally. His advice on how to relate with fear or pain or groundlessness was to welcome it, to become one with it rather than split ourselves in two, one part of us rejecting or judging another part. His instruction on how to relate with the breath was to touch it lightly and let it go. His instruction on how to relate with the thoughts was the same: leave them free to dissolve back into space without making meditation into a self-improvement project.

The attitude toward meditation presented here is one of relaxing. With no feeling of striving to reach some higher state, we simply sit down and, without a goal, without trying to become peaceful or get rid of all thoughts, we stay faithful to the instructions: sitting comfortably, eyes open, be precisely yet lightly aware of the meditation object (it's not tight concentration), and when mind wanders off, gently come back. Whatever occurs, we do not congratulate or condemn ourselves. The image often used is of an old person, sitting in the sun, watching children at play, with an attitude of nothing left to do.

Naturally, we are wise to be patient with this process and give ourselves unlimited time. It's as if we've been kicking a spinning wheel all our life and it has its own momentum. It's spinning rapidly, but now finally we're learning how to stop kicking the wheel. We can expect that the wheel is going to keep spinning for some time. It won't just abruptly stop. This is where many of us find ourselves: we've stopped kicking the wheel, we're not always strengthening the habit, but we're in this interesting middle state, somewhere between not always caught and not always able to resist biting the hook. This is called "the spiritual path." In fact, this path is all there is. How we relate moment by moment to what is happening on the spot is all there really is. We give up all hope of fruition and in the process we just keep learning what it means to appreciate being right here.

A few years ago I was overwhelmed by deep anxiety, a fundamental, intense anxiety with no storyline attached. I felt very vulnerable, very afraid and raw. While I sat and breathed with it, relaxed into it, stayed with it, the terror did not abate. It was unrelenting even after many days, and I didn't know what to do.

I went to see my teacher Dzigar Kongtrül, and he said, "Oh, I know that place." That was reassuring. He told me about times in his life when he had been caught in the same way. He said it had been an important part of his journey and had been a great teacher for him. Then he did something that shifted how I practice. He asked me to describe what I was experiencing. He asked me where I felt it. He asked me if it hurt physically and if it were hot or cold. He asked me to describe the quality of the sensation, as precisely as I could. This detailed exploration continued for a while and then he brightened up and said, "Ani Pema, that's the Dakini Bliss. That's a high level of spiritual bliss." I almost fell off my chair. I thought, "Wow, this is great!" And I couldn't wait to feel that intensity again. And do you know what happened? When I eagerly sat down to practice, of course, since the resistance was gone, so was the anxiety.

I now know that at a nonverbal level the aversion to my experience had been very strong. I had been making the sensation bad. Basically, I just wanted it to go away. But when my teacher said "Dakini bliss," it completely changed the way I looked at it. So that's what I learned: Take an interest in your pain and your fear. Move closer, lean in, get curious; even for a moment experience the feelings beyond labels, beyond being good or bad. Welcome them. Invite them. Do anything that helps melt the resistance.

Then the next time you lose heart and you can't bear to experience what you're feeling, you might recall this instruction: change the way you see it and lean in. That's basically the instruction that Dzigar Kongtrül gave me. And I now pass it on to you. Instead of blaming our discomfort on outer circumstances or on our own weakness, we can choose to stay present and awake to our experience, not rejecting it, not grasping it, not buying the stories that we relentlessly tell ourselves. This is priceless advice that addresses the true cause of suffering—yours, mine, and that of all living beings.

SEVEN

REJOICING IN THINGS AS
THEY ARE

W HEN WE BEGIN TO SEE CLEARLY WHAT WE DO, HOW
we get hooked and swept away by old habits, our usual
tendency is to use that as a reason to get discouraged, a reason
to feel really bad about ourselves. Instead, we could realize how
remarkable it is that we actually have the capacity to see ourselves
honestly, and that doing this takes courage. It is moving in the direction of seeing our life as a teacher rather than as a burden. This
involves, fundamentally, learning to stay present, but learning to
stay with a sense of humor, learning to stay with loving-kindness
toward ourselves and with the outer situation, learning to take
joy in the magic ingredient of honest self-reflection. Chögyam
Trungpa called this "making friends with ourselves." This friendship is based on knowing all parts of ourselves without prejudice.
It's an unconditional friendliness.

Learning to stay is the basis for connecting with natural warmth;
it is the basis for loving ourselves and also for compassion. The more
you stay present with yourself, the more you realize what all of us
are up against. Just like me, other people feel pain and want it to
go away. Just like me, they go about this in a way that only makes
matters worse.

When we start to see the chain reaction of shenpa, it's not as if
we then feel superior about this achievement. Instead, this insight
has the potential to humble us and cause us to have more sympathy for other people's confusion. When we see someone else

getting hooked and swept away, instead of automatically being irritated, we have more chance of recognizing our sameness. We are definitely all in the same boat, and knowing this can make us very forgiving.

In the Buddhist teachings on compassion there's a practice called "one at the beginning, and one at the end." When I wake up in the morning, I do this practice. I make an aspiration for the day. For example, I might say, "Today, may I acknowledge whenever I get hooked." Or, "May I not speak or act out of anger." I try not to make it too grandiose, as in, "Today, may I be completely free of all neurosis." I begin with a clear intention, and then I go about the day with this in mind.

In the evening, I review what happened. This is the part that can be so loaded for Western people. We have an unfortunate tendency to emphasize our failures. But when Dzigar Kongtrül teaches about this, he says that for him, when he sees that he has connected with his aspiration even once briefly during the whole day, he feels a sense of rejoicing. He also says that when he recognizes he lost it completely, he rejoices that he has the capacity to see that. This way of viewing ourselves has been very inspiring for me.

He encourages us to ask what it is in us, after all, that sees that we lost it. Isn't it our own wisdom, our own insight, our own natural intelligence? Can we just have the aspiration, then, to identify with the wisdom that acknowledges that we hurt someone's feelings, or that we smoked when we said we wouldn't? Can we have the aspiration to identify more and more with our ability to recognize what we're doing instead of always identifying with our mistakes? This is the spirit of delighting in what we see rather than despairing in what we see. It's the spirit of letting compassionate self-reflection build confidence rather than becoming a cause for depression.

Being able to acknowledge shenpa, being able to know that we are getting stuck, this is the basis of freedom. Just being able to recognize what's happening without denial—we should rejoice in that. Then, if we can take the next step and refrain from going down the same old road, which sometimes we'll be able to do and sometimes we won't, we can rejoice that sometimes we do have that ability to interrupt the momentum—that "sometimes" is major progress.

We can rejoice when we are able to acknowledge and refrain, and also we should expect relapses. Sometimes it's one step forward, one step back. Then maybe one step forward, a half step back. When people do the Weight Watchers program, they're told that their weight will go up and down, that they're not always going to be losing those pounds. It's recommended to be patient with weight loss, and that when you gain weight over one week, it's no problem. You're asked to look at it from the bigger perspective, to pay attention to what happens over a month or over many months.

It's like that when we work with our firmly entrenched habits, as well. We include the compassionate realization that people have relapses. Chögyam Trungpa gave a teaching about this. He said that if we had nothing but smooth sailing, if our habitual patterns just dropped away, continually, week after week with no problem, we would have no empathy for all those people who continue to get hooked and act out.

He said the ideal spiritual journey needs the balance of "gloriousness" and "wretchedness." If it were all glory, just one success after another, we'd get extremely arrogant and completely out of touch with human suffering. On the other hand, if it were all wretchedness and we never had any insights, and never experienced joy or inspiration, then we'd get so discouraged that we'd give up. So, what's needed is a balance. But as a species, we tend to overemphasize the wretchedness.

For instance, when we review our day, it's common to perceive it all as bleak, as if we didn't get anything right. But maybe if somebody else is there, a partner for example, he or she might say, "What about the fact that you were getting all worked up, and you went out for a walk and came back calmed down?" Or, "I saw you smile at that man who was sitting in the corner all hunched over and depressed, and I saw him brighten up." Sometimes other people have to point this out to us.

In our most ordinary days we have moments of happiness, moments of comfort and enjoyment, moments of seeing something that pleased us, something that touched us, moments of contacting the tenderness of our hearts. We can take joy in that. I find that it's essential during the day to actually note when I feel happiness or when something positive happens, and begin to cherish those moments as precious. Gradually we can begin to cherish the preciousness of our whole life just as it is, with its ups and downs, its failures and successes, its roughness and smoothness.

Until we start this journey of acknowledging when we're being hooked, little things unconsciously trigger us all the time. The slightest setback or annoyance will trigger us and we'll be blind to what's going on. Life just becomes increasingly more of a struggle and we never can figure out why.

Once we start seeing, of course we still get triggered, but there's a very important difference: the magic of recognition, the miracle of compassionate acknowledgment. It's the miracle of being conscious rather than unconscious. The more we do it, the more our ability to do it grows. That's not something we have to force. It just naturally happens that when there's less self-deception, we have an increased capacity to remain awake to the joys and sorrows of the world.

It doesn't help at all to feel guilty about where we find ourselves. When we can shed the light of compassionate attention on our actions, an interesting shift can happen—this regret of ours becomes a seed of compassion for all the other people just like us who are caught in fixed mind, closed mind, hard heart. We let this recognition connect us with others. We let it be the seed of empathy, and we go forward, not wallowing in guilt and shame about what we did.

In *The Art of Happiness*, Howard Cutler asked the Dalai Lama if there was anything he's done in his life that he felt bad about, anything he regretted. He said there was and told the story of an older monk who came to see him one day and asked about doing a certain high-level Buddhist practice. The Dalai Lama casually told the old man that this practice would be difficult and perhaps would be better undertaken by someone who was younger, that traditionally it was a practice that should be started in one's teens. He later found out that the monk killed himself in order to be reborn in a younger body to more effectively undertake the practice.

Cutler was stunned. He asked the Dalai Lama how he had been able to deal with his regret. He also asked how he had gotten rid of it. The Dalai Lama paused for a long time and really thought about it. Then he said, "I didn't get rid of it. It's still here." He went on to say, "Even though that feeling of regret is still here, it isn't associated with a feeling of heaviness or a quality of pulling me back."

I was very moved by that. We have this mistaken idea that either we have regret or we get rid of it. Trungpa Rinpoche talked about holding the sadness of life in our heart while never forgetting the beauty of the world and the goodness of being alive. There comes a time when we are able to be pierced to the heart by our own suffering, and the suffering of others, and by our own regrets, without it dragging us down. The Dalai Lama went on to say that being dragged down by regrets or held back by them would be to no one's benefit, so he learns from his mistakes and goes forward doing all he can to help others. I think we could say he is the great teacher that he is because of how he works with his own challenges. It's not as though he goes through life untouched, with no sadness or remorse. But he doesn't turn this into what we call "guilt," or the shame that drags us down and makes us feel powerless to be there for ourselves or anybody else.

This possibility is not just available to people like the Dalai Lama. It's waiting for any of us, every moment of every day. When we look back to our last moment, our last hour, our last day, if we can say that we caught ourselves when we were hooked and interrupted the momentum, if this was true even briefly, we can rejoice. And if we didn't realize what was happening, and once again acted in an old familiar way, we can rejoice that we have the ability, the wisdom, to be conscious and actually acknowledge that, and go forward—perhaps older, wiser, and more compassionate for having made mistakes, for having had relapses.

EIGHT

UNCOVERING NATURAL OPENNESS

NOTHING IS STATIC AND PERMANENT. AND THAT IN-cludes you and me. We know this about cars and carpets, new shirts and DVD players, but are less willing to face it when it comes to ourselves or to other people. We have a very solid view of ourselves, and also very fixed views about others. Yet if we look closely, we can see that we aren't even slightly fixed. In fact, we are as unfixed and changing as a river. For convenience, we label a constant flow of water the Mississippi or the Nile, very much the way we call ourselves Jack or Helen. But that river isn't the same for even a fraction of a second. People are equally in flux—I am like that, and so are you. Our thoughts, emotions, molecules are continually changing.

If you are inclined to train in being open-endedly present to whatever arises—to life's energy, to other people, and to this world—after a while you'll realize you're open and present to something that's not staying the same. For example, if you are truly open and receptive to another person, it can be quite a revelation to realize that they aren't exactly the same on Friday as they were on Monday, that each of us can be perceived freshly any day of the week. But if that person happens to be your parent or sibling, your partner or your boss, you are usually blinded and see them as predictably always the same. We have a tendency to label one another as an irritating person, a bore, a threat to our happiness and security, as inferior or superior; and this goes way beyond our close circle of acquaintances at home or at work.

This labeling can lead to prejudice, cruelty, and violence; and in any time or place when prejudice, cruelty, and violence occur, whether it's directed by one being toward another or by groups of beings toward other groups, there's a theme that runs through: "This person has a fixed identity, and they are *not like me*." We can kill someone or we can be indifferent to the atrocities perpetrated on them because "they're just hajis," or "they're just women," or "they're just gay." You can fill in the blank with any racial slur, any dehumanized label that's ever been used for those we consider different.

There's a whole other way to look at one another—and that is to try dropping our fixed ideas and get curious about the possibility that nothing and no one remains always the same. This starts, of course, with getting curious and dropping the limiting stories we've created about ourselves. Then we have to stay present with whatever is happening to us. What I find helpful is to think of whatever I am experiencing—whether it's sadness, anger, or worry; pleasure, joy, or delight—as simply the dynamic, fluid energy of life as it is manifesting right now. That shifts the resistance I have to my experience. Because I've been practicing this approach for some years now, I've come to have confidence in the capacity for open receptivity, for wakefulness and nobility, in all beings. And I've seen that how we regard and treat one another can draw this nobility out.

In the book *The Search for a Nonviolent Future* by Michael Nagler there's a story that illustrates this. It concerns a Jewish couple, Michael and Julie Weisser—but it could have been any victim of prejudice and violence. The Weissers were living in Lincoln, Nebraska, where Michael had a prominent role at the synagogue, and Julie was a nurse. In 1992 they began to receive threatening phone calls and notes from the Ku Klux Klan. Of course this was illegal at the time and not condoned in this town, but nevertheless it was happening. The police told them that it was probably the work of Larry Trapp. He was the Grand Dragon, the head of the Klan, in that town. Michael and Julie Weisser knew of Trapp's reputation as a man filled with hatred. And they knew that he was in a wheelchair, having been disabled by a beating years ago.

Each day, Larry's voice on the phone would threaten to kill them, destroy their property, and harm their family and friends. Then one day Michael decided, just on the spot with the support of Julie, to try something. So in the next phone call, when Larry Trapp was ranting at them, he waited for an opportunity to speak. He knew that Trapp had a hard time getting around in his wheelchair, so when he could get a word in, he offered him a ride to the grocery store. Trapp didn't speak for a while, and when he did, the anger had left his voice. He said, "Well, I've got that taken care of, but thanks for asking."

By then, the Weissers had more in mind than ending the harassment: they wanted to help free Larry Trapp from the torment of his prejudice and rage. They began calling *him*, and told him if he needed help, they would be there for him. Not long after that they went to his apartment, taking him a home-cooked dinner, and the three of them got to know one another better. And he did begin to ask them for help. One day when they arrived for a visit, Trapp took off the ring he wore and gave it to them. It was a Nazi ring. With that gesture he was breaking his association with the Ku Klux Klan, telling the Weissers, "I denounce everything they stand for. But it's not the people in the organizations that I hate. . . . If I were to say I hate all Klansmen because they're Klansmen . . . I would still be a racist." Rather than replacing one prejudice with another, Larry Trapp chose to let go of closed-mindedness altogether.

Like Larry Trapp, each of us has our own capacity for prejudice, and it's very common to justify it when it comes up. Our fixed ideas about "them" arise quickly, and this has again and again caused great suffering. This is a very old habit, a crippling habit, a universal response to feeling threatened. We can look at this habit with compassion and openness but not continue to reinforce and strengthen it. Instead, we can acknowledge the powerful energy of our fear, of our rage—the energy of anything at all that we may feel—as the natural movement of life, and become intimate with it, abide with it, without repressing, without acting out, without letting it destroy us or anyone else. In this way, anything we experience becomes the perfect opportunity for touching our basic goodness, the perfect support for remaining open and receptive to the dynamic energy of life. As radical as this idea might seem, I know it to be true that there is nothing that can occur that has to set off the chain reaction of shenpa. Anything we experience, no matter how challenging, can become an open pathway to awakening.

Sometimes in a really threatening situation there may not be a lot we can do or say to help anyone, but we can always train in staying present and not biting the hook. I received a letter from my friend Jarvis Masters, an inmate on death row, recently in which he told me that there are many times when the prison atmosphere is so violent that all he can do is not harm anybody and not get caught up in the seductive force of aggression. The stories don't always have a happy ending.

If you're in a profession where you're interacting with violent people, you know that it's not so easy to avoid getting hooked. But we could ask: "How can I regard the ones I don't agree with, with an open mind?" "How can I look deeper, listen deeper, than my fixed ideas?" or "How can I address the ones who are in a cycle of violence, the people who are hurting others, as living, feeling human beings just like me?" We know that if we approach anyone with our fixed preconceptions, with our minds and hearts already closed, then we'll never be able to communicate genuinely, and we can easily exacerbate the situation and promote more suffering.

Underlying hatred, underlying any cruel act or word, underlying all dehumanizing, there is always fear—the utter groundlessness of fear. This fear has a soft spot. It hasn't frozen yet into a solid position. However much we don't like it, fear doesn't have to give birth to aggression or the desire to harm ourselves or others. When we feel fear or anxiety or any groundless feeling, or when we realize that the fear is already hooking us into "I'm going to get even" or "I have to go back to my addiction to escape this," then we can regard the moment as neutral, a moment that can go either way. We are presented all the time with a choice. Do we return to old destructive habits or do we take whatever we're experiencing as an opportunity and support for having a fresh relationship with life?

Basic wakefulness, natural openness, is always available. This openness is not something that needs to be manufactured. When we pause, when we touch the energy of the moment, when we slow down and allow a gap, self-existing openness comes to us. It does not require a particular effort. It is available anytime. As Chögyam Trungpa once remarked, "Openness is like the wind. If you open your doors and windows, it is bound to come in."

The next time you're getting worked up, experiment with looking at the sky. Go to the window, if you have one in your home or office, and look up at the sky. I once read an interview with a man who said that during the Second World War, he survived internment in a Japanese concentration camp by looking at the sky and seeing the clouds still drifting there and the birds still flying there. This gave him trust that the goodness of life would go on despite the atrocities that he was witnessing.

Usually when we're all caught up, we're so engrossed in our storyline that we lose our perspective. The painful situation at home, in our job, in prison, in war, wherever we might find ourselves—when we're caught in the difficulty, our perspective usually becomes very narrow, microscopic even. We have the habit of automatically going inward. Taking a moment to look at the sky or taking a few seconds to abide with the fluid energy of life, can give us a bigger perspective—that the universe is vast, that we are a tiny dot in space, that endless, beginningless space is always available to us. Then we might understand that our predicament is just a moment in time, and that we have a choice to strengthen old habitual responses or to be free. Being open and receptive to whatever is happening is always more important than getting worked up and adding further aggression to the planet, adding further pollution to the atmosphere.

Whatever occurs is the right opportunity to shift the basic tendency to get hooked, to get worked up, to close our minds and hearts. Whatever we perceive or feel or think is the perfect support for making a fundamental shift toward openness. Natural openness has the power to give life meaning and to inspire us. With just a moment of recognition that the natural openness is here, gradually you realize that natural intelligence and natural warmth are present too. It's like opening a door to the vastness and timelessness and magic of the place in which you find yourself.

When you are waking up in the morning and you aren't even out of bed, even if where you are is frightening or perhaps so routine that it's boring or deadening, you could look out and take three conscious breaths. Just be where you are. When you are standing in a line waiting, just allow for a gap in your discursive mind. You can look at your hands and breathe, you can look out the window or down the street or up at the sky. It doesn't matter if you look out or if you give your full attention to a detail. You can let the experience be a contrast to being all caught up, let it be like popping a bubble, a moment in time, and then you just go on.

When you meditate, every time you realize that you are thinking and you let the thoughts go, that openness is available. Chögyam Trungpa called it being "free from fixed mind." Every time the breath goes out into space, that openness is available. In any moment you could put your full attention on the immediacy of your experience, you could look at the floor or the ceiling, or just feel your bottom sitting on the chair. Do you see what I mean? You can just be here. Instead of being not here, instead of being caught up, absorbed in thinking, planning, worrying—caught in the cocoon where you're cut off from your sense perceptions, cut off from the sounds and the sights, cut off from the power and magic of the moment—instead of that you could choose to pause. When you go out for a walk in the country, in the city, anywhere at all, just stop now and then. Punctuate your life with these moments.

In modern life, it's so easy to get consumed, particularly by computers and TVs and cell phones. They have a way of hypnotizing us. As long as we are on automatic pilot, just run around by our thoughts and emotions, we'll feel overwhelmed. It doesn't make much difference whether we're at a peaceful meditation center or in the busiest, most caught-up place in the world. In any setting, we can allow a gap and let natural openness come to us. Over and over and over, we can allow the space to realize where we are, to realize how vast our mind is. Find a way to slow down. Find a way to relax your mind and do it often, very, very often, throughout the day, not just when you are hooked but all the time.

The crucial point is that we can relate with our life just as it is right now, not later when things improve. We can always connect with the openness of our minds. We can use our days to wake up rather than go back to sleep. Give this approach a try. Make a commitment to pausing throughout the day, and do that whenever you can. Allow time for your perception to shift. Allow time to experience the natural energy of life as it is manifesting right now. This can bring dramatic changes in your personal life, and if you are worried about the state of the world, this is a way that you can use every moment to help shift the global climate of aggression toward peace.

NINE

THE IMPORTANCE OF PAIN

B EFORE WE CAN KNOW WHAT NATURAL WARMTH REALLY
is, often we must experience loss. We go along for years moving through our days, propelled by habit, taking life pretty much
for granted. Then we or someone dear to us has an accident or
gets seriously ill, and it's as if blinders have been removed from
our eyes. We see the meaninglessness of so much of what we do
and the emptiness of so much we cling to.

When my mother died and I was asked to go through her personal belongings, this awareness hit me hard. She had kept boxes
of papers and trinkets that she treasured, things that she held on
to through her many moves to smaller and smaller accommoda-
tions. They had represented security and comfort for her, and
she had been unable to let them go. Now they were just boxes of
stuff, things that held no meaning and represented no comfort or
security to anyone. For me these were just empty objects, yet she
had clung to them. Seeing this made me sad, and also thoughtful.
After that I could never look at my own treasured objects in the
same way. I had seen that things themselves are just what they
are, neither precious nor worthless, and that all the labels, all our
views and opinions about them, are arbitrary.

This was an experience of uncovering basic warmth. The loss
of my mother and the pain of seeing so clearly how we impose
judgments and values, prejudices, likes and dislikes, onto the
world, made me feel great compassion for our shared human
predicament. I remember explaining to myself that the whole

world consisted of people just like me who were making much ado about nothing and suffering from it tremendously.

When my second marriage fell apart, I tasted the rawness of grief, the utter groundlessness of sorrow, and all the protective shields I had always managed to keep in place fell to pieces. To my surprise, along with the pain, I also felt an uncontrived tenderness for other people. I remember the complete openness and gentleness I felt for those I met briefly in the post office or at the grocery store. I found myself approaching the people I encountered as just like me—fully alive, fully capable of meanness and kindness, of stumbling and falling down and of standing up again. I'd never before experienced that much intimacy with unknown people. I could look into the eyes of store clerks and car mechanics, beggars and children, and feel our sameness. Somehow when my heart broke, the qualities of natural warmth, qualities like kindness and empathy and appreciation, just spontaneously emerged.

People say it was like that in New York City for a few weeks after September 11. When the world as they'd known it fell apart, a whole city full of people reached out to one another, took care of one another, and had no trouble looking into one another's eyes.

It is fairly common for crisis and pain to connect people with their capacity to love and care about one another. It is also common that this openness and compassion fades rather quickly, and that people then become afraid and far more guarded and closed than they ever were before. The question, then, is not only how to uncover our fundamental tenderness and warmth but also how to abide there with the fragile, often bittersweet vulnerability. How can we relax and open to the uncertainty of it?

The first time I met Dzigar Kongtrül, he spoke to me about the importance of pain. He had been living and teaching in North America for over ten years and had come to realize that his students took the teachings and practices he gave them at a superficial level until they experienced pain in a way they couldn't shake. The Buddhist teachings were just a pastime, something to dabble in or use for relaxation, but when their lives fell apart, the teachings and practices became as essential as food or medicine.

The natural warmth that emerges when we experience pain includes all the heart qualities: love, compassion, gratitude, tenderness in any form. It also includes loneliness, sorrow, and the shakiness of fear. Before these vulnerable feelings harden, before the storylines kick in, these generally unwanted feelings are pregnant with kindness, with openness and caring. These feelings that we've become so accomplished at avoiding can soften us, can transform us. The open-heartedness of natural warmth is sometimes pleasant, sometimes unpleasant—as "I want, I like" and as the opposite. The practice is to train in not automatically fleeing from uncomfortable tenderness when it arises. With time we can embrace it just as we would the comfortable tenderness of lovingkindness and genuine appreciation.

A person does something that brings up unwanted feelings, and what happens? Do we open or close? Usually we involuntarily shut down, yet without a storyline to escalate our discomfort we still have easy access to our genuine heart. Right at this point we can recognize that we are closing, allow a gap, and leave room for change to happen. In Jill Bolte Taylor's book *My Stroke of Insight,* she points to scientific evidence showing that the life span of any particular emotion is only one and a half minutes. After that we have to revive the emotion and get it going again.

Our usual process is that we automatically *do* revive it by feeding it with an internal conversation about how another person is the source of our discomfort. Maybe we strike out at them or at someone else—all because we don't want to go near the unpleasantness of what we're feeling. This is a very ancient habit. It allows our natural warmth to be so obscured that people like you and me, who have the capacity for empathy and understanding, get so clouded that we can harm each other. When we hate those who activate our fears or insecurities, those who bring up unwanted feelings, and see them as the sole cause of our discomfort, then we can dehumanize them, belittle them, and abuse them.

Understanding this, I've been highly motivated to make a practice of doing the opposite. I don't always succeed, but year by year I become more familiar and at home with dropping the storyline and trusting that I have the capacity to stay present and receptive to other beings. Suppose you and I spent the rest of our lives doing this? Suppose we spent some time every day bringing the unknown people that we see into focus, and actually taking an interest in them? We could look at their faces, notice their clothes, look at their hands. There are so many chances to do this, particularly if we live in a large town or in a city. There are panhandlers that we rush by because their predicament makes us uncomfortable, there are the multitudes of people we pass on streets and sit next to on buses and in waiting rooms. The relationship becomes more intimate when someone packs up our groceries or takes our blood pressure or comes to our house to fix a leaking pipe. Then there are the people who sit next to us on airplanes. Suppose you had been on one of the planes that went down on September 11. Your fellow passengers would have been very important people in your life.

It can become a daily practice to humanize the people that we pass on the street. When I do this, unknown people become very real for me. They come into focus as living beings who have joys and sorrows just like mine, as people who have parents and neighbors and friends and enemies, just like me. I also begin to have a heightened awareness of my own fears and judgments and prejudices that pop up out of nowhere about these ordinary people that I've never even met. I've gained insight into my sameness with all these people, as well as insight into what obscures this understanding and causes me to feel separate. By increasing our awareness of our strength as well as our confusion, this practice uncovers natural warmth and brings us closer to the world around us.

When we go in the other direction, when we remain self-absorbed, when we are unconscious about what we are feeling and blindly bite the hook, we wind up with rigid judgments and fixed opinions that are throbbing with shenpa. This is a setup for closing down to anyone who threatens us. To take a common example, how do you feel about people who smoke? I haven't found too many people, either smokers or nonsmokers, who are shenpa-free on this topic. I was once in a restaurant in Boulder, Colorado, when a woman from Europe who didn't realize you couldn't smoke inside, lit up. The restaurant was noisy, bustling with conversation and laughter, and then she lit her cigarette. The sound of the match striking caused the whole place to stop. You could hear yourself breathe, and the righteous indignation in the room was palpable.

I don't think it would have gone over very well with the crowd if I had tried to point out that in many places in the world smoking is not viewed negatively and that their shenpa-filled value judgments, not this smoker, were the real cause of their discomfort.

When we see difficult circumstances as a chance to grow in bravery and wisdom, in patience and kindness, when we become more conscious of being hooked and we don't escalate it, then our personal distress can connect us with the discomfort and unhappiness of others. What we usually consider a problem becomes the source of empathy. Recently a man told me that he devotes his life to trying to help sex offenders because he knows what it's like to be them. As a teenager he sexually abused a little girl. Another example is a woman I met who said that as a child she had hated her brother so violently that she thought of ways to kill him every day. This now allows her to work compassionately with juveniles who are in prison for murder. She can work with them as her equals because she knows what it's like to stand in their shoes.

The Buddha taught that among the most predictable human sufferings are sickness and old age. Now that I'm in my seventies I understand this at a gut level. Recently I watched a movie about a mean-spirited seventy-five-year-old woman whose health was failing and whose family didn't like her. The only kindness in her life came from her devoted border collie. For the first time in my life I identified with the old lady rather than her children. This was a major shift: a whole new world of understanding, a new area of sympathy and kindness, had suddenly been revealed to me.

This can be the value of our personal suffering. We can understand firsthand that we are all in the same boat and that the only thing that makes any sense is to care for one another.

When we feel dread, when we feel discomfort of any kind, it can connect us at the heart with all the other people feeling dread and discomfort. We can pause and touch into dread. We can touch the bitterness of rejection and the rawness of being slighted. Whether we are at home or in a public spot or caught in a traffic jam or walking into a movie, we can stop and look at the other people there and realize that in pain and in joy they are just like me. Just like me they don't want to feel physical pain or insecurity or rejection. Just like me they want to feel respected and physically comfortable.

When you touch your sorrow or fear, your anger or jealousy, you are touching everybody's jealousy, you are knowing everybody's fear or sorrow. You wake up in the middle of the night with an anxiety attack and when you can fully experience the taste and smell of it, you are sharing the anxiety and fear of all humanity and all animals as well. Instead of your distress becoming all about you, it can become your link with everyone all over the world who is in the same predicament. The stories are different, the causes are different, but the experience is the same. For each of us sorrow has exactly the same taste; for each of us rage and jealousy, envy and addictive craving have exactly the same taste. And so it is with gratitude and kindness. There can be two zillion bowls of sugar, but they all have the same taste.

Whatever pleasure or discomfort, happiness or misery you are experiencing, you can look at other people and say to yourself, "Just like me they don't want to feel this kind of pain." Or, "Just like me they appreciate feeling this kind of contentment."

When things fall apart and we can't get the pieces back together, when we lose something dear to us, when the whole thing is just not working and we don't know what to do, this is the time when the natural warmth of tenderness, the warmth of empathy and kindness, are just waiting to be uncovered, just waiting to be embraced. This is our chance to come out of our self-protecting bubble and to realize that we are never alone. This is our chance to finally understand that wherever we go, everyone we meet is essentially just like us. Our own suffering, if we turn toward it, can open us to a loving relationship with the world.

TEN

UNLIMITED FRIENDLINESS

I'VE OFTEN HEARD THE DALAI LAMA SAY THAT HAVING compassion for oneself is the basis for developing compassion for others. Chögyam Trungpa also taught this when he spoke about how to genuinely help others, how to work for the benefit of others without the interference of our own agendas. He presented this as a three-step process. Step one is *maitri*, a Sanskrit word meaning loving-kindness toward all beings. Here, however, as Chögyam Trungpa used the term, it means unlimited friendliness toward ourselves, with the clear implication that this leads naturally to unlimited friendliness toward others. *Maitri* also has the meaning of trusting oneself—trusting that we have what it takes to know ourselves thoroughly and completely without feeling hopeless, without turning against ourselves because of what we see.

Step two in the journey toward genuinely helping others is communication from the heart. To the degree that we trust ourselves, we have no need to close down on others. They can evoke strong emotions in us but still we don't withdraw. Based on this ability to stay open, we arrive at step three, the difficult-to-come-by fruition: the ability to put others before ourselves and help them without expecting anything in return.

When we build a house, we start by creating a stable foundation. Just so, when we wish to benefit others, we start by developing warmth or friendship for ourselves. It's common, however, for people to have a distorted view of this friendliness and warmth. We'll say, for instance, that we need to take care of ourselves, but how many of us really know how to do this? When clinging to security and comfort and warding off pain become the focus of our lives, we don't end up feeling cared for and we certainly don't feel motivated to extend ourselves to others. We end up feeling more threatened or irritable, more unable to relax.

I've known many people who have spent years exercising daily, getting massages, doing yoga, faithfully following one food or vitamin regimen after another, pursuing spiritual teachers and different styles of meditation, all in the name of taking care of themselves. Then something bad happens to them and all those years don't seem to have added up to the inner strength and kindness for themselves that they need to relate with what's happening. And they don't add up to being able to help other people or the environment. When taking care of ourselves is all about me, it never gets at the unshakable tenderness and confidence that we'll need when everything falls apart. When we start to develop maitri for ourselves, unconditional acceptance of ourselves, then we're really taking care of ourselves in a way that pays off. We feel more at home with our own bodies and minds and more at home in the world. As our kindness for ourselves grows, so does our kindness for other people.

The peace that we are looking for is not peace that crumbles as soon as there is difficulty or chaos. Whether we're seeking inner peace or global peace or a combination of the two, the way to experience it is to build on the foundation of unconditional openness to all that arises. Peace isn't an experience free of challenges, free of rough and smooth, it's an experience that's expansive enough to include all that arises without feeling threatened.

I sometimes wonder how I would respond in an emergency. I hear stories about people's bravery emerging in crises, but I've also heard some painful stories from people who weren't able to reach out to others in need because they were so afraid for themselves. We never really know which way it will go. So I ponder what would happen, for instance, if I were in a situation where there was no food but I had a bit of bread. Would I share it with the others who were starving? Would I keep it for myself? If I contemplate this question when I'm feeling the discomfort of even mild hunger, it makes the process more honest. The reality gets through to me that if I give away all my food, then the hunger I'm feeling won't be going away. Maybe another person will feel better, but for sure physically I will feel worse.

Sometimes the Dalai Lama suggests not eating one day a week or skipping a meal one day a week to briefly put ourselves in the shoes of those who are starving all over the world. In practicing this kind of solidarity myself, I have found that it can bring up panic and self-protectiveness. So the question is, what do we do with our distress? Does it open our heart or close it? When we're hungry, does our discomfort increase our empathy for hungry people and animals, or does it increase our fear of hunger and intensify our selfishness?

With contemplations like this we can be completely truthful about where we are but also aware of where we'd like to be next year or in five years, or where we'd like to be by the time we die. Maybe today I panic and can't give away even a crumb of my bread, but I don't have to sink into despair. We have the opportunity to lead our lives in such a way that year by year we'll be less afraid, less threatened, and more able to spontaneously help others without asking ourselves, "What's in this for me?"

A fifty-year-old woman told me her story. She had been in an airplane crash at the age of twenty-five. She was in such a panic rushing to get out of the plane before it exploded, that she didn't stop to help anyone else, including, most painfully, a little boy who was tangled in his seat belt and couldn't move. She had been a practicing Buddhist for about five years when the accident happened; it was shattering to her to see how she had reacted. She was deeply ashamed of herself, and after the crash she sank into three hard years of depression. But ultimately, instead of her remorse and regret causing her to self-destruct, these very feelings opened her heart to other people. Not only did she become committed to her spiritual path in order to grow in her ability to help others, but she also became engaged in working with people in crisis. Her seeming failure is making her a far more courageous and compassionate woman.

Right before the Buddha attained enlightenment under the bodhi tree, he was tempted in every conceivable way. He was assaulted by objects of lust, objects of craving, objects of aggression, of fear, of all the variety of things that usually hook us and cause us to lose our balance. Part of his extraordinary accomplishment was that he stayed present, on the dot, without being seduced by anything that appeared. In traditional versions of the story, it's said that no matter what appeared, whether it was demons or soldiers with weapons or alluring women, he had no reaction to it at all. I've always thought, however, that perhaps the Buddha *did* experience emotions during that long night, but recognized them as simply dynamic energy moving through. The feelings and sensations came up and passed away, came up and passed away. They didn't set off a chain reaction. This process is often depicted in paintings as weapons transforming into flowers—warriors shooting thousands of flaming arrows at the Buddha as he sits under the bodhi tree but the arrows becoming blossoms. That which can cause our destruction becomes a blessing in disguise when we let the energies arise and pass through us over and over again, without acting out.

A question that has intrigued me for years is this: how can we start exactly where we are, with all our entanglements, and still develop unconditional acceptance of ourselves instead of guilt and depression?

One of the most helpful methods I've found is the practice of compassionate abiding. This is a way of bringing warmth to unwanted feelings. It is a direct method for embracing our experience rather than rejecting it. So the next time you realize that you're hooked, you could experiment with this approach.

Contacting the experience of being hooked, you breathe in, allowing the feeling completely and opening to it. The in-breath can be deep and relaxed—anything that helps you to let the feeling be there, anything that helps you not push it away. Then, still abiding with the urge and edginess of feelings such as craving or aggression, as you breathe out you relax and give the feeling space. The out-breath is not a way of sending the discomfort away but of ventilating it, of loosening the tension around it, of becoming aware of the space in which the discomfort is occurring.

This practice helps us to develop maitri because we willingly touch parts of ourselves that we're not proud of. We touch feelings that we think we shouldn't be having—feelings of failure, of shame, of murderous rage; all those politically incorrect feelings like racial prejudice, disdain for people we consider ugly or inferior, sexual addiction, and phobias. We contact whatever we're experiencing and go beyond liking or disliking by breathing in and opening. Then we breathe out and relax. We continue that for a few moments or for as long as we wish, synchronizing it with the breath. This process has a leaning-in quality. Breathing in and leaning in are very much the same. We touch the experience, feeling it in the body if that helps, and we breathe it in.

In the process of doing this, we are transmuting hard, reactive, rejecting energy into basic warmth and openness. It sounds dramatic, but really it's very simple and direct. All we are doing is breathing in and experiencing what's happening, then breathing out as we continue to experience what's happening. It's a way of working with our negativity that appreciates that the negative energy per se is not the problem. Confusion only begins when we can't abide with the intensity of the energy and therefore spin off. Staying present with our own energy allows it to keep flowing and move on. Abiding with our own energy is the ultimate nonaggression, the ultimate maitri.

Compassionate abiding is a stand-alone practice, but it can also serve as a preliminary for doing the practice of *tonglen,* the practice of taking in and sending out. Tonglen is an ancient practice designed to short-circuit "all about me." Just as with compassionate abiding, the logic of the practice is that we start by breathing in and opening to feelings that threaten the survival of our self-importance. We breathe in feelings that generally we want to get rid of. On the out-breath of tonglen, we send out all that we find pleasurable and comfortable, meaningful and desirable. We send out all the feelings we usually grasp after and cling to for dear life.

Tonglen can begin very much like compassionate abiding. We breathe in anything we find painful and we send out relief, synchronizing this with the breath. Yet the emphasis with tonglen is always on relieving the suffering of others. As we breathe in discomfort, we might think, "May I feel this completely so that I and all other beings may be free of pain." As we breathe out relief, we might think, "May I send out this contentment completely so that all beings may feel relaxed and at home with themselves and with the world." In other words, tonglen goes beyond compassionate abiding because it is a practice that includes the suffering of other beings and the longing that this suffering could be removed.

Tonglen develops further as your courage to experience your own unwanted feelings grows. For instance, when you realize you're hooked, you breathe in with the understanding, even if it's only conceptual at first, that this experience is shared by every being and that you aspire to alleviate their suffering. As you breathe out, you send relief to everyone. Still, your direct experience, the experience you're tasting right now, is the basis for having any idea at all about what other beings go through. In this way tonglen is a heart practice, a gut-level practice, not a head practice or intellectual exercise.

It's common for parents of young children to spontaneously put their children first. When little ones are ill, mothers and fathers often have no problem at all wishing they could take away the child's suffering; they would gladly breathe it in and take it away if they could, and they would gladly breathe out relief.

It's suggested to start tonglen with situations like that where it's fairly easy. The practice becomes more challenging when you start to do it for people you don't know, and almost impossible when you try to do it for people you don't like. You breathe in the suffering of a panhandler on the street and aren't sure you want to. And how willing are you to do more advanced tonglen where you breathe in the pain of someone you despise and send them relief? From our current vantage point, this can seem too much to ask, too overwhelming or too absurd.

The reason why tonglen practice can be so difficult is because we can't bear to feel the feelings that the street person or our nemesis bring up in us. This, of course, brings us back to compassionate abiding and making friends with ourselves. It has been precisely this process of doing tonglen, trying to stretch further and open my mind to a wider and wider range of people, that has helped me to see that without maitri I will always close down on other people when certain feelings are provoked.

The next time you have a chance, go outside and try to do tonglen for the first person you meet, breathing in their discomfort and sending out well-being and caring. If you're in a city, just stand still for a while and pay attention to anyone who catches your eye and do tonglen for them. You can begin by contacting any aversion or attraction or even a neutral uninterested feeling that they bring up in you, and breathe in, contacting that feeling much as you do with compassionate abiding but with the thought, "May both of us be able to feel feelings like this without it causing us to shut down to others." As you breathe out, send happiness and contentment to them. If you encounter an animal or person who is clearly in distress, pause and breathe in with the wish that they be free of their distress and send out relief to them. With the most advanced tonglen you breathe in with the wish that you could actually take on their distress so they could be free of it and you breathe out with the wish that you could give them all your comfort and ease. In other words you would literally be willing to stand in their shoes and have them stand in yours if it would help.

By trying this, we learn exactly where we are open and where we are closed. We learn quickly where we would do well to just practice abiding compassionately with our own confused feelings, before we try to work with other people, because right now our efforts would probably make a bigger mess. I know many people who want to be teachers, or feed the homeless, or start clinics, or try in some way to truly help others. Despite their generous intentions they don't always realize that if they plan to work closely with people, they may be in for a lot of shenpa. The people they hope to help will not always see them as saviors. In fact they will probably criticize them and give them a hard time. Teachers and helpers of all kinds will be of limited use if they are doing their work to build up their own egos. In fact, setting out to help others is a very quick way to pop the bubble of ego.

So, we start by making friends with our experience and developing warmth for our good old selves. Slowly, very slowly, gently, very gently, we let the stakes get higher as we touch in on more troubling feelings. This leads to trusting that we have the strength and good-heartedness to live in this precious world, despite its land mines, with dignity and kindness. With this kind of confidence, connecting with others comes more easily, because what is there to fear when we have stayed with ourselves through thick and thin? Other people can provoke anything in us and we don't need to defend ourselves by striking out or shutting down. Selfless help, helping others without an agenda, is the result of having helped ourselves. We feel loving toward ourselves and therefore we feel loving toward others. Over time all those we used to feel separate from become more and more melted into our heart.

TAKING THIS INTO THE WORLD

D EEP DOWN IN THE HUMAN SPIRIT THERE IS A RESERVOIR of courage. It is always available, always waiting to be discovered.

In the last years of his life, Chögyam Trungpa taught unceasingly on the very real possibility of creating enlightened society—a society where individuals cultivated unconditional friendliness for themselves and unconditional caring for others. It is true that when we try to do either of these things, we find that it's not so easy. The resistance to accepting ourselves and to putting others' welfare first is surprisingly strong. Nevertheless, he spoke with enthusiasm and confidence about our remarkable capacity for bravery, for open-mindedness, for tenderness—our remarkable capacity to be spiritual warriors, fearless men and women who can help to heal the sorrows of the world.

The Buddhist master Shantideva set forth a path for training in spiritual warriorship. In his text *The Way of the Bodhisattva,* he explains how the bodhisattva or spiritual warrior begins the journey by looking honestly at the current state of his or her mind and emotions. The path of saving others from confusion starts with our willingness to accept ourselves without deception.

You would think that a training whose intention was to prepare us to benefit others would focus exclusively on other people's needs. But the majority of Shantideva's instructions entail working skillfully with our own blind spots. Until we do this, we are in the dark about how other people feel and what might soothe them. It only dawns on us slowly that the way sorrow and joy feel to me is the same way they feel to others. As Shantideva put it, since every single being on the earth feels insecurity and pain, just the way I do, then why do I keep putting the emphasis only on me?

This book has been an attempt to look closely at how we stay stuck in this kind of narrow, self-absorbed vision. It has also been an attempt to pass on some of what my teachers have taught me about how to get unhooked. The motivation for presenting this material, however, is not solely the wish that each of us might become happier. The primary intention is that we might follow the advice contained here in order to prepare ourselves to look beyond our own welfare and consider the great suffering of others and the fragile state of our world. As we change our own dysfunctional habits, we are simultaneously changing society. Our own awakening is intertwined with the awakening of enlightened society. If we can lose our personal appetite for aggression and addiction, the whole planet will rejoice.

For the sake of all sentient beings, I hope that you will join the growing society of aspiring and full-fledged spiritual warriors who are emerging from every continent on the globe. May we never give up our genuine concern for the world. May our lives become a training ground for awakening our natural intelligence, openness, and warmth, and may this small text be of some support on the way. As Chögyam Trungpa joyfully proclaimed, "We can do it!"

ACKNOWLEDGMENTS

I want to express my gratitude to the women who helped me bring this book to fruition. My thanks go to Eden Steinberg for envisioning the book, to Glenna Olmsted and Angela Rose for their secretarial support, to Martha Boesing for her insightful comments, and especially to Sandy Boucher, my friend and editor, who so beautifully shaped the transcripts into their final form.

RELATED READINGS

Brach, Tara. *Radical Acceptance: Embracing Your Life with the Heart of a Buddha*. New York: Bantam Books, 2003.

Chödrön, Pema. *No Time to Lose: A Timely Guide to the Way of the Bodhisattva*. Boston: Shambhala Publications, 2005.

Kongtrül, Dzigar. *It's Up to You: The Practice of Self-Reflection on the Buddhist Path*. Boston and London: Shambhala Publications, 2005.

————. *Light Comes Through: Buddhist Teachings on Awakening to Our Natural Intelligence*. Boston and London: Shambhala Publications, 2008.

Masters, Jarvis Jay. *Finding Freedom: Writings from Death Row*. Junction City, Calif.: Padma Publishing, 1997.

Nagler, Michael N. *The Search for a Nonviolent Future: A Promise of Peace for Ourselves, Our Families, and Our World*. Novato, Calif.: New World Library, 2004.

Shantideva, *The Way of the Bodhisattva*. Translated by Padmakara Translation Group. Boston: Shambhala Publications, 1997.

Trungpa, Chögyam. *Shambhala: The Sacred Path of the Warrior*. Boston: Shambhala Publications, 1984, 1988.

————. *Great Eastern Sun: The Wisdom of Shambhala*. Boston: Shambhala Publications, 1999.

RESOURCES

For information about meditation instruction or to find a practice center near you, please contact one of the following:

SHAMBHALA MEDITATION CENTERS
1084 Tower Road
Halifax, NS B3H 2Y5
Canada
phone: (902) 470-1118
fax: (902) 423-2750
website: www.shambhala.org

SHAMBHALA EUROPE
Kartäuserwall 20
50678 Köln
Germany
phone: 49-221-31024-00
fax: 49-221-31024-50
e-mail: office@shambhala-europe.org
website: www.shambhala-europe.org

KARMÊ CHÖLING
369 Patneaude Lane
Barnet, Vermont 05821
phone: (802) 633-2384
fax: (802) 633-3012

e-mail: reception@karmecholing.org
website: www.karmecholing.org

SHAMBHALA MOUNTAIN CENTER
151 Shambhala Way
Red Feather Lakes, Colorado 80545
phone: (970) 881-2184
fax: (970) 881-2909
e-mail: info@shambhalamountain.org
website: www.shambhalamountain.org

GAMPO ABBEY
Pleasant Bay
Cape Breton, NS B0E 2P0
Canada
phone: (902) 224-2752
e-mail: office@gampoabbey.org
website: www.gampoabbey.org

Naropa University is the only accredited, Buddhist-inspired university in North America. For more information, contact:

NAROPA UNIVERSITY
2130 Arapahoe Avenue
Boulder, Colorado 80302
phone: (303) 444-0202
e-mail: info@naropa.edu
website: www.naropa.edu

Audio and video recordings of talks and seminars by Pema Chödrön are available from:

The Pema Chödrön Foundation
PO Box 770630
Steamboat Springs, Colorado 80477
phone: (607) 738-5232
e-mail: tim@pemachodronfoundation.org
website: www.pemachodronfoundation.org

Kalapa Recordings
2178 Gottingen Street
Halifax, NS B3K 3B4
Canada
phone: (888) 450-1002
e-mail: recordings@shambhala.org
website: www.kalapamedia.com

Sounds True
413 S. Arthur Avenue
Louisville, Colorado 80027
phone: (800) 333-9185
e-mail: info@soundstrue.com
website: www.soundstrue.com

Heart Advice: Weekly Quotes from Pema Chödrön

Visit shambhala.com/pemaheartadvice to sign up for Heart Advice and receive words of wisdom from Pema Chödrön to your inbox once a week!

ABOUT THE AUTHOR

Pema Chödrön is an American Buddhist nun in the lineage of Chögyam Trungpa, the renowned Tibetan meditation master. She is resident teacher at Gampo Abbey, Cape Breton, Nova Scotia, the first Tibetan monastery in North America established for Westerners. She is the author of several books, including the best-selling *When Things Fall Apart* and *The Places That Scare You*.

THE PEMA CHÖDRÖN
FOUNDATION

All of the author's proceeds from the sale of this book go to The
Pema Chödrön Foundation. The Pema Chödrön Foundation supports Pema's own monastery, Gampo Abbey, and the develop-
ment of the monastic tradition in the West. Monastic life is based
on training within a community of others who have committed
themselves to the goal of awakening the dignity and wisdom that
is the human inheritance of all.

For more information, or to make a tax-deductible contribu-
tion, please visit www.pemachodronfoundation.org/how-to-help.
Donations can also be sent to:

THE PEMA CHÖDRÖN FOUNDATION
P.O. Box 770630
Steamboat Springs, CO 80477

BOOKS AND AUDIO BY PEMA CHÖDRÖN

BOOKS

Awakening Loving-Kindness

We often look far and wide for guidance to become better people, as though the answers were *somewhere out there*. But Pema Chödrön suggests that the best and most direct teacher for awakening loving-kindness is in fact *your very own life*. Based on talks given during a one-month meditation retreat at Gampo Abbey, where Pema lives and teaches, her teachings here focus on learning how to see the events of our lives as the perfect material for learning to love ourselves and our world playfully and wholeheartedly— and to live in our skin fearlessly, without aggression, harshness, or shame.

Becoming Bodhisattvas: A Guidebook for Compassionate Action

The Way of the Bodhisattva has long been treasured as an indispensable guide to enlightened living, offering a window into the greatest potential within us all. Written in the eighth century by the scholar and saint Shantideva, it presents a comprehensive view of the Mahayana Buddhist tradition's highest ideal—to commit oneself to the life of a bodhisattva warrior, a person who is wholeheartedly dedicated to the freedom and common good of all beings. In this comprehensive commentary, Pema Chödrön invites you to journey more deeply into this liberating way of life, presenting Shantideva's text verse-by-verse and offering both illuminating stories and practical exercises to enrich the text and bring its timeless teachings to life in our world today.

Comfortable with Uncertainty: 108 Teachings on Cultivating Fearlessness and Compassion

Collecting some of the most powerful passages from Pema Chödrön's many beloved books, this compact handbook for spiritual practice is rich with inspiration and insight. Here she explores life-changing concepts, themes, and practices from the Buddhist tradition, showing how anyone (not just Buddhists) can draw from them to become more courageous, aware, and kindhearted. It includes the benefits of meditation and mindfulness, letting go of the fixations that weigh us down, working directly with fear and other painful emotions, and much more.

The Compassion Book

Here Pema Chödrön introduces a powerful, transformative practice called *lojong*, which has been a primary focus of her teachings and personal practice for many years. This book presents fifty-nine pithy slogans from the *lojong* teachings for daily contemplation and includes Pema's clear, succinct guidance on how to understand them—and how they can enrich our lives. It also features a forty-five minute downloadable audio program entitled "Opening the Heart."

Living Beautifully with Uncertainty and Change

We live in difficult times. Life sometimes seems like a roiling and turbulent river threatening to drown us and destroy the world. Why, then, shouldn't we cling to the certainty of the shore—to our familiar patterns and habits? Because, Pema Chödrön teaches, that kind of fear-based clinging keeps us from the infinitely more satisfying experience of being fully alive. The teachings she presents here—known as the "Three Commitments"—provide a wealth of wisdom for learning to step right into the river: to be completely, fearlessly present even in the hardest times, the most difficult situations.

The Places That Scare You: A Guide to Fearlessness in Difficult Times

We always have a choice in how we react to the circumstances of our lives. We can let them harden us and make us increasingly resentful and afraid, or we can let them soften us and allow our inherent human kindness to shine through. Here Pema Chödrön provides essential tools for dealing with the many difficulties that life throws our way, teaching us how to awaken our basic human goodness and connect deeply with others—to accept ourselves and everything around us complete with faults and imperfections. If we go to the places that scare us, Pema suggests, we just might find the boundless life we've always dreamed of.

The Pocket Pema Chödrön

This treasury of 108 short selections from the best-selling books of Pema Chödrön offers teachings on breaking free of destructive patterns; developing patience, kindness, and joy amid our everyday struggles; becoming fearless; and unlocking our natural warmth, intelligence, and goodness. Designed for on-the-go inspiration, this is a perfect guide to Buddhist principles and the foundations of meditation and mindfulness.

Practicing Peace

In this pocket-size guide to the practice of inner peace, Pema Chödrön shows us how to look deeply at the underlying causes of our tensions and how we really *can* create a more peaceful world—by starting right where we are and learning to see the seeds of hostility in our hearts. She draws on Buddhist teachings to explore the origins of anger, aggression, hatred, and war, and offers practical techniques all of us can use to work for genuine, lasting peace in our own lives and in whatever circumstances we find ourselves.

Start Where You Are: A Guide to Compassionate Living

Pema here offers down-to-earth guidance on how we can go beyond the fleeting attempts to "fix" our pain and, instead, to take our lives as they are as the only path to achieve what we all yearn for most deeply—to embrace rather than deny the difficulties of our lives. These teachings, framed around fifty-nine traditional Tibetan Buddhist maxims, point us directly to our own hearts and minds, such as "Always meditate on whatever provokes resentment," "Be grateful to everyone," and "Don't expect applause." By working with these slogans as everyday meditations, *Start Where You Are* shows how we can all develop the courage to work with our own inner pain and discover true joy, holistic well-being, and unshakeable confidence.

Taking the Leap: Freeing Ourselves from Old Habits and Fears

These classic Buddhist teachings about *shenpa* (painful attachments and compulsions) help us see how certain habits of mind tend to "hook" us and get us stuck in states of anger, blame, self-hatred, and addiction—and how we can liberate ourselves from them. Pema offers insights and practices we can immediately put to use in our lives to take a bold leap toward a new way of living—one that will bring about positive transformation for ourselves and for our troubled world.

When Things Fall Apart: Heart Advice for Difficult Times

How can we live our lives when everything seems to fall apart—when we are continually overcome by fear, anxiety, and pain? The answer, Pema Chödrön suggests, might be just the opposite of what you expect. Here, in her most beloved and acclaimed work, Pema shows that moving *toward* painful situations and becoming intimate with them can open up our hearts in ways we never before imagined. Drawing from traditional Buddhist wisdom, she offers life-changing tools for transforming suffering and negative patterns into habitual ease and boundless joy.

The Wisdom of No Escape: And the Path of Loving-Kindness
In this guide to true kindness for self and others, Pema Chödrön presents a uniquely practical approach to opening ourselves up to life in all circumstances. She reveals that when we embrace the happiness and heartache, inspiration and confusion, and all the twists and turns that are a natural part of life, we can begin to discover a true wellspring of courageous love that's been within our hearts all along.

AUDIO

Be Grateful to Everyone: An In-Depth Guide to the Practice of Lojong
One of the best ways to bring meditation off the cushion and into everyday life is to practice *lojong* (or mind training). For centuries, Tibetans have used fifty-nine powerful mind-training slogans as a way to transform life's ordinary situations into opportunities for awakening. Pema Chödrön here presents her definitive audio teachings on *lojong*. She offers an overview of the practice and goes on to provide inspiring commentary on the slogans while paying special attention to how to apply them on the spot in our daily lives.

Comfortable with Uncertainty: 108 Teachings on Cultivating Fearlessness and Compassion
This audiobook offers short, stand-alone teachings designed to help us cultivate compassion and awareness amid the challenges of daily living. More than a collection of thoughts for the day, *Comfortable with Uncertainty* offers a progressive program of spiritual study, leading the reader through essential concepts, themes, and practices on the Buddhist path.

Don't Bite the Hook: Finding Freedom from Anger, Resentment, and Other Destructive Emotions

In this recorded weekend retreat, Pema draws on Buddhist teachings to show us how to relate constructively to the inevitable shocks, losses, and frustrations of life so that we can find true happiness. The key, Pema explains, is not biting the "hook" of our habitual responses.

The Fearless Heart: The Practice of Living with Courage and Compassion

Pema shows us how to transform negative emotions like fear and guilt into courageous self-acceptance in *The Fearless Heart*. Her teachings are based on five aphorisms presented to Machig Lapdronma, one of Tibetan Buddhism's greatest female teachers. Pema offers insightful guidance on how to remain courageous in the face of pain, and how to increase feelings of generosity and passion through fearlessness. This audio program includes an extensive question-and-answer session and guided meditation practices available for the first time.

Fully Alive: A Retreat with Pema Chödrön on Living Beautifully with Uncertainty and Change

In this recorded weekend retreat, Pema Chödrön and her teaching assistant, Meg Wheatley, teach us to stop clinging to the certainty of life's shore and to instead step right into the river: to be completely, fearlessly present, even in the hardest times, the most difficult situations. That's the secret of being fully alive.

Giving Our Best: A Retreat with Pema Chödrön on Practicing the Way of the Bodhisattva

Pema Chödrön here teaches on how to nurture a compassionate attitude, using a text that is very close to her heart: the Buddhist classic known as *The Way of the Bodhisattva*. She focuses on its primary subject, the enlightened heart and mind (*bodhicitta*), showing us how this awakened state, which often seems infinitely far out of our grasp, is always available to us right where we are.

Perfect Just as You Are: Buddhist Practices on the Four Limitless Ones—Loving-Kindness, Compassion, Joy, and Equanimity

Here are Pema Chödrön's definitive teachings on the Buddhist practice called the "Four Limitless Ones"—a practice that helps us recognize and grow the seeds of love, compassion, joy, and equanimity already present in our hearts. This in-depth study course offers: guided meditations, on-the-spot practices to use in the midst of daily life, an overview of *bodhichitta* and the bodhisattva vow, guided shamatha meditation, writing and reflection exercises, methods to weaken the grip of negative emotions, and question-and-answer sessions.

Practicing Peace in Times of War: Four Talks

The book *Practicing Peace* is based on several of Pema Chödrön's public talks, and we are proud to present them to you here, in this audio edition. It is a short, pithy, and profound work that includes practical strategies for cultivating the seeds of peace and compassion amid life's upsets and challenges.

Smile at Fear: A Retreat with Pema Chödrön on Discovering Your Radiant Self-Confidence

Behind each of our fears resides a basic fear of *ourselves*. In this recorded retreat, Pema Chödrön shares teachings inspired by the book *Smile at Fear*, which was written by her teacher Chögyam Trungpa. Here is a vision for moving beyond this most basic fear of self to discover the innate bravery, trust, and joy that reside at the core of our being.

Start Where You Are: A Guide to Compassionate Living

With insight and humor, Pema Chödrön offers guidance on how we can accept our flaws and embrace ourselves wholeheartedly as a prerequisite for developing compassion. Through working with fifty-nine Tibetan Buddhist slogans, Pema shows us how to develop the courage to face our inner pain and thereby discover a wealth of freedom, well-being, and confidence.

This Moment Is the Perfect Teacher: Ten Buddhist Teachings on Cultivating Inner Strength and Compassion

Lojong is a powerful Tibetan Buddhist practice created especially for training the mind to work with the challenges of everyday living. It teaches our hearts to soften, reframes our attitude toward difficulty, and allows us to discover a wellspring of inner strength. In this recorded retreat, Pema Chödrön introduces the lojong teachings and explains how we can apply them to any situation in our life—because, as Pema says, "every moment is an opportunity for awakening."

When Things Fall Apart: Heart Advice for Difficult Times

This abridged audiobook based on the beloved spiritual classic contains radical and compassionate advice for what to do when our lives become painful and difficult. Read by Pema, it includes instructions on how to use painful emotions to cultivate wisdom, compassion, and courage; how to communicate in a way that leads to openness and true intimacy with others; and how to reverse negative habitual patterns.

The Wisdom of No Escape: And the Path of Loving-Kindness

It's true, as they say, that we can love others only when we first love ourselves, and we can experience real joy only when we stop running from pain. The key to understanding these truisms lies in remaining open to life in all circumstances, and here Pema Chödrön shows us how.